God Unknown

Ian Mobsby is an Anglican priest currently licensed in the Diocese of London to the Guild Church of St Mary Aldermary and the Moot Community, with over twenty years' experience researching and working with new forms of Church. He is a founder member of two small missional communities, including the Moot Community in central London. He is also an Associate Missioner of the Archbishops' Fresh Expressions team, a member of the Church of England's College of Evangelists and a national selector for Ordained Pioneer Ministry. As a writer and teacher Ian lectures extensively in the UK, USA, Canada, Australia and New Zealand. As an enthusiast of new monasticism in the UK, he is a member of the Church of England's Advisory Council for Religious Communities and Diocesan Bishops, assisting the Church at a national level to nurture and develop small missional communities.

God Unknown

*The Trinity in Contemporary
Spirituality and Mission*

Ian Mobsby

CANTERBURY
PRESS
Norwich

© Ian Mobsby 2008, 2012

This edition published in 2012 by the Canterbury Press Norwich
Editorial office
13–17 Long Lane,
London, EC1A 9PN, UK

Canterbury Press is an imprint of Hymns Ancient & Modern Ltd
(a registered charity)
13A Hellesdon Park Road, Norwich,
Norfolk, NR6 5DR, UK

Published in 2008 by YTC Press under the title *The Becoming of G-d*

www.canterburypress.co.uk

Scripture quotations are from the New Revised Standard Version of the Bible,
copyright 1989 by the Division of Christian Education of the National Council
of the Churches of Christ in the USA. Used by permission. All rights reserved.

British Library Cataloguing in Publication data

A catalogue record for this book is available
from the British Library

978 1 84825 170 0

Originated by The Manila Typesetting Company
Printed and bound by
CPI Group (UK) Ltd., Croydon, CR0 4YY

Contents

In grateful memory of Gladys Mary Plant
and Sarah Plant.
You were both greatly loved, and now
greatly missed.

Preface

In 2006 I had the privilege of publishing my MA Dissertation, 'Emerging & Fresh Expressions of Church', through Moot Community Publishing. In that study, essentially an investigation into the theology of Emerging and Fresh Expressions of church, I came across for the first time the incredible depth of Trinitarian informed Christian ecclesiology. The research phase of the study, from 2002 to 2005, was a delightful time of discovery of the deep connection between the Holy Trinity and contemporary experimental expressions of church in an increasingly post-secular context. My continued involvement in the Moot Community in London, and the various lectures and talks I have since given, have provided me ample opportunity to experience and explore Trinitarianism more fully.

This book, now in its second rewritten published form, attempts to reflect on the spiritual implications of the Trinity, and in particular the theology of the Cappadocian Mothers and Fathers who were so influential in helping to conceptualize it. The writing process has been a wonderful journey of discipleship and self-discovery. For the first time I have had the opportunity to explore the concepts such as perichoresis, kenosis, panentheism and *theosis*, all of which interrelate and have profound implications for the Church in the twenty-first century. I have been greatly challenged by the work of Colin Gunton, in particular his book *Becoming and Being*. A chapter of this book is named in honour of Gunton's work.

The Trinity has been a key motif of my own spiritual journey with God for at least the last ten years, and my constant preoccupation

ix

with the implications of a deeply Trinitarian understanding of God has at times driven my friends completely mad. So I want to give thanks to all my friends for their tolerance and support during this project, particularly in the last three years.

My grateful thanks go to Katherine Venn, Aaron Kennedy and Jonny Spoor, who are much better detail people than I will ever be. Thanks also to Mike Radcliffe for the contribution of his icon and poetry, and to all those acknowledged in the devotional chapter concerning the Trinity and prayer. Finally, thanks to Christine Smith and Canterbury Press for being willing to publish this much improved exploration into the mystery that is God.

It is my hope that this book can in some small way point to the depth of spirituality in Trinitarian theology, aiding and encouraging post-secular pilgrims to dig deep within the Christian tradition to find sustenance and meaning for the journey.

Introduction

Trinitarian theology simply winds some people up, and for many good reasons. For centuries it has been used to promote male-dominated, hierarchical and controlling approaches to church structures and the Christian faith. In this form Trinitarianism has been used to exclude, persecute, kill and prevent interfaith under-standing in favour of dominance and control. However, this is not the full story. The late twentieth century has seen movements such as liberation theology reframe the concept of 'God's-oneness-in-community' to instigate a mission focused on justice and social inclusion. I believe God continues to speak through the paradoxical concept of the Trinity, and that it will prove particularly perti-nent for those seeking to re-imagine what it means to be church, and Christian, in the twenty-first century. Our main challenge is to still our hearts and tune our ears to the quiet voice with which the Spirit speaks. We need to attend to the voice of God amid the cacophony of competing voices at large in our culture, in an effort to nurture spiritual communities that can then become profound places of God. The odds are perhaps stacked against us, but the rewards of distinctly Christian, contextual expressions of worship, mission and community will be rich.

The Trinitarian God

Central to the Christian faith is the paradox that God is One, but is expressed in three persons. This view is held central in most Christian churches and traditions. God then is One – but also Father, Son and Holy Spirit. In more functional and gender-inclusive understandings, the Trinity has been expressed as Creator, Redeemer and Sustainer or Counsellor. Christianity is unique in the world religions for holding this view of God's One-ness in three persons.

Why is this important? Now more than ever we see a Western culture that seeks relationship and belonging but fears it in equal measure. Our post-Reformation, post-Enlightenment inheritance is the cult of the individual, and in short we desire community but often have no idea how to seek it. As a result, our culture has become less humane. The Church has not escaped the scourge of rampant individualism. Some churches operate like depersonalized corporate companies, emphasizing the 'business' of conversion; others operate like imperialistic establishments, where a certain façade of self-sufficiency is kept in place at all times. Both forms of individualism gravely impoverish the quality of our spiritual communities. Trinitarian theology, I would suggest, is a key to recovering a depth of relationship we have been missing for so long.

It has been said that we live in a 'post-secular' culture. Whatever the full import of this term, it is clear that personally, spiritually and religiously, these are complex times. Religion it seems is under pressure, while 'spirituality' has emerged as its less institutional, more eclectic successor. The last century also saw the rise of various fundamentalisms – an approach to life that seeks to simplify complexity by means of rigid edifices of rational, logical thought-systems. Unfortunately these are often deeply dehumanizing and devaluing of real community and the relational. Moreover, vio-

Post-secularization

When looking at history, sociologists often talk of epochs or world-views to define social change. In recent history, these have been defined as premodernity, modernity, postmodernity and post-secularization. Premodernity is the world-view before the Enlightenment and the rise of science, which led into modernity and the Age of Reason. Postmodernity and Post-secularization denote a further change of world-view and cultural change after modernity. Secularization is the process of reducing religious, spiritual and philosophical belief in general society. Post-secularization denotes a time when the forces of secularization have not only stopped, but where social forces have driven a renewed appreciation for the place of spirituality in general society. Whether post-secularization is actually ongoing is hotly contested. It is my contention that it is not only happening, but here to stay.

lence and oppression often go hand in hand with fundamentalism, in and outside of the Church.

It is into this mix that the vibrancy of the Trinity speaks to us, drawing us into intentional forms of relationship that change and challenge us to the core of our being. Who is it that we seek when we seek the Lord our God? How does this three-in-one God transform our way of life? How do we live in a strange land where we need to learn social skills, tolerance and love? What will inspire us to shift from being semi-skilled spiritual tourists, to committed and passionate Christian pilgrims? It is my belief, and the substance of this book, that God is seeking to draw us into deeper forms of spiritual community and relationship through God's own experientially revealed nature. The challenge to the Church then is whether it is willing to listen to the still, small voice of the God who, like it or not, never stands still.

1

Knowing God: Rational and Trans-rational

'Logic is the beginning of wisdom . . . not the end.'
Dr Spock, Star Trek VI: The Undiscovered Country

Like many 'Generation Xers' born in the late 1960s, my childhood was a rich mix of family, atheism and scientific rationalism. I was brought up to mistrust religion as the 'opiate of the masses', as something that controlled people through guilt and misdirected power. Going to church was what you occasionally did because, for your family's sake, you had to attend baptisms, weddings and funerals. Although I was extremely shy, I loved my wider family which I remember as a mix of passionate arguments about politics, beach rounders, swimming and picnics. Wisdom and knowledge were strictly about deductive thinking and reasoning. Knowledge was about facts and reasoned argument, and religion was little more than superstition and wearing outdated clothes. However, there was a deep contradiction. This same family was also extremely artistic, with a love of music and the arts. Yet this form of artistic or intuitive 'knowledge' was largely ignored.

Things were different for me: the arts touched my emotions and a deeper sense of self, and enabled me to see a legitimate place for spirituality; and from an early age my experience of and delight in the world enabled me to transcend my family's belief in atheism. These glimpses of the Divine, or rather 'knowing through artistic experiences', began with my sitting in our back garden encountering nature. My mother tells me that as a child I would sit for hours listening to birdsong and the sound of bees and insects, smelling flowers and trees, and sensing the warmth of the sun. Looking back I am sure that I encountered the Divine first through nature.

My next important memory, and first real spiritual experience, was contemplating the Chagall stained-glass window in Chichester Cathedral. I loved that church building – it was full of mystery, beauty and awe. Chagall's window was an overpowering experience of bright colours and symbolism, which deeply moved me. Near to this, in the shrine to St Richard of Chichester, was an image of the Trinity that to me made perfect sense. I experienced God as Trinity to be a mystical truth: something I just knew to be true, even though I had little experience or understanding of Christianity.

So what has this got to do with the Holy Trinity? Well it starts with the question 'how do we know what we know?' For a very long time we in the Western world have constructed our beliefs predominantly by reason and argument. We have neglected knowing through artistic experience, contemplation or intuition. Only recently have we begun to realize that a more healthy answer to the question is a balance of knowing through both reason and experience.

It is therefore unsurprising that in an age of scientific rationalism, when knowing through artistic and spiritual experience is neglected, the Church has struggled to communicate the Holy Trinity as the key defining and distinctive expression of the Christian God. I do not believe you can ever really understand the Trinity by learning facts alone; you ultimately need to experience God as Trinity to 'know' that it is true.

St Francis of Assisi was once challenged by a number of questioners on the detail of the Nicene Creed, the nature of the Trinity and why he believed what he did. He was reportedly astonished that they had asked such a question, because he quite literally experienced the Holy Trinity through daily contemplative prayer.

Ultimately then, we 'know what we know' through logic *and* experience. For too long we have overplayed the importance of facts, logic and science, and undervalued the contribution of emotional experience, reflection and 'gut feeling'. This form of knowing is not through the head, but rather through the heart. To understand the full implications of the Holy Trinity, we need to *experience* God as well as know facts about God.

One of the mysteries of being human is that we tend to be either 'head' or 'heart' people. Rarely are we both. Yet to deeply understand the Holy Trinity, to be true disciples of God, we need to draw on both head and heart.

For the sake of ease, I want to call logical and fact-based knowing 'rational', and experiential, intuitive knowing 'trans-rational'. Those who are more 'rational' (knowing through the head) tend to be scientists, philosophers or scientific rationalists. Those who are more 'trans-rational' (knowing through the heart) tend to be artists, creatives, poets, musicians and – importantly, in this discussion – those interested in spirituality and contemplative pursuits such as meditation. Rationalists tend to see trans-rationalists as superstitious, overly subjective and emotional. Trans-rationalists tend to see rationalists as arrogant, cold and emotionally unintelligent. The truth is that we need both the rational and the trans-rational to fully engage with Christian spirituality. I truly believe that you cannot understand the Holy Trinity unless you have a 'both–and' approach to knowing. You will have an impoverished understanding of the Trinity if your understanding is based solely on doctrine or facts, and similarly you will have an ill-defined understanding of the Trinity if it is all about poetry or the prayerful experience of God. So the challenge for us in the twenty-first century, and as we begin to explore the implications of the Triune God in this book, is to take a both–and rational and trans-rational approach.

Only in this both–and way (which is a form of non-dualism) will we ever make sense of the doctrines of the Christian faith. How can Mary the Mother of God be both a virgin and a mother? How can the Trinity be one yet three, and still one?

No one in my family has ever really understood my faith, no matter how much I have tried to express my experience of God.

I have failed miserably to translate my trans-rational experience into a compelling rational argument that they could relate to. This is because rational words can never fully articulate the peace and love of God that I have experienced in prayer and daily life; I can never fully express this in words.

With a purely rational or dualistic approach to knowledge, a deep Christian spirituality can be neither fully comprehended nor processed. Scientific rationalism has no way of understanding paradox, and so reduces it to little more than superstition. Only by holding the trans-rational and rational together, in non-dualistic thinking, can you fully comprehend paradox. And the Trinitarian nature of God is surely the ultimate expression of spiritual paradox!

In Western civilization this dualism – the battle between head and heart, between the rational and the trans-rational – has led to the creation of a divide between the sacred and the secular.

The battle continues today, with atheists such as Richard Dawkins and others sparring with articulate exponents in the Church, who deliver clever arguments based on a purely rational understanding of faith. Ultimately the debate will never be won either way, as spiritual knowing can never be fully articulated through rational argument alone. In fact, many people in contemporary culture are seeking new solutions to the problems they face through non-rational approaches to knowing. Please do not mishear me by thinking I am against debate and dialogue; quite the opposite. But I do not think the Christian path can be communicated solely through rational argument. Many have tried, many with moments of brilliance. But if C. S. Lewis could not ultimately succeed, I most certainly will never be able to do so.

This distortion brought about by dualism has dominated our shared Western consciousness, but at the same time many people have sensed that a purely rational knowing cannot incorporate everything. Deep questions of life have not yet been answered; mystery and paradox are still alive. And so we have come to realize that logic is only one aspect of human knowing. To quote *Star Trek's* Dr Spock: 'Logic is the beginning of wisdom . . . not the end.'

Now that we have entered a time of great danger, with the threat of ecological catastrophe and global economic insecurity, many people are reawakening to another way of knowing, which comes out of ancient reasoning and experience, out of wisdom, out of the contemplative and the prayerful. This approach requires us to live with questions. We cannot problem-solve our way out of every predicament, but must rather seek the sacred, the whole, the common good beyond the individual ego and the mind. As we follow the spiritual path, the more we discover, the more many of us realize that we do not know.

Trans-rationality, then, is an act of intellectual modesty that states that rational knowing can only take you so far. To go beyond the limit of rationalism we need other means of knowing, through art, wisdom, experience, intuition and spiritual encounter. Yes, there is still an important place for rationalism in religion and spirituality – knowing facts about God – but the foundation of faith, knowing God through the *experience* of God, trans-rationalism, needs to be at the heart of faith or the spiritual path. Knowing through personal experience is a vital form of trans-rationalism that we are now rediscovering.

To be able to explore and fully comprehend the doctrine of the Trinity, we need to draw on a certain amount of trans-rationalism, so that we ourselves experience the truth of the Triune God. Yes, we need to know certain facts about the Trinity, but its importance, and the incredible wisdom found in Trinitarian thinking, needs to be experienced. Only then will we open up the heart of Christianity and, through it, our shared humanity.

Trans-rational thinking resonates with contemporary culture, and ancient modes of knowing, such as the contemplative approach (experiencing God from within, the practice of meditation and deep prayer), have once again become a key approach to living and knowing.

It is with this trans-rational approach that we can now re-engage with the Trinity, and more fully appreciate the implications of a Trinitarian-informed faith and spirituality. For too long, knowing

God through the experience of God has been treated as inferior to reasoning about God. This book seeks to redress this balance, so that experience is equal to reason in how we process knowing God. Taking a both–and non-dualistic approach opens us all up to the heart of faith – an encounter with God that leads to understanding in cycles of experience, faith and doubt, and then further experience, faith and doubt. This is not new; I would argue that this has always been the authentic spiritual path of Christian discipleship, right back to its Hebrew roots.

Sacramental

The gift or grace of God; God's presence through us; signs and symbols such as icons, bread and wine.

So the implications of the Trinity, sacramental, contemplative and mysterious, become accessible to a culture that reaches beyond the purely rational.

The Trinity shows us what both true spirituality and the real meaning of Christianity are all about: God gathering a community of autonomous individuals that collectively become one, and thus participation in mystery, belonging and unending love. It shows us a God that is both absent and present, this-worldly yet other-worldly, a God that is immeasurable and uncontrollable yet knowable.

So this return to mystery is a vital call, inspiring a new humility, an approach to knowing that begins in our not-knowing, not blinded by our ego, anger, fear or pride. It was, after all, for just such reasons that the scientific method was itself sometimes found to be subjective. Scientists as human beings can also be skewed by the sins of self-interest. Much has been written on how the scientific method under-appreciates human individual self-interest, which can skew supposedly objective results. It is with great hope that I see our culture shifting from a secular culture to a post-secular one, including the re-emergence of trans-rational thinking alongside the rational.

I am hopeful that engagement with both the doctrine and experience of the Holy Trinity can once again become a resource for Christianity in a culture that is increasingly nihilistic, consumerist and defined by an unrestrained global market. In this way the Trinity can stand as a life-giving and hopeful authoritative central concept, not unlike *sola scriptura* ('by scripture alone') in the time of the Reformation. I hope that the spiritual searchers of our day, increasingly curious about God and spirituality, are more open to experience and exploring the Triune God through contemplative Christian events and services, along with the possibility of dialogue and scriptural exploration.

The Bible is a great source for trans-rational wisdom. It is important to remember that most of its content was originally meant to be heard and not read individually. Storytelling, the medium of much of the Old and New Testaments, is an ancient form of knowing through imaginative experiential encounter. The master of this was Jesus Christ himself. In many of the Gospel stories, Jesus is challenged by the crowds, Scribes and Pharisees by questions of belief and morality. Most of these questions were articulated in a strongly rationalist way. Some were constructed to try and trip Jesus into a conceptual trap. With a brilliance that could only come from the Divine, Jesus answered rationalist questions with trans-rational parables. The parables are a form of metaphorical story that use ordinary characters and situations, but with a symbolic twist that then brings unexpected meaning through subjective imaginative engagement. They begin by reinforcing the individual's world-view, then add an unexpected element that challenges the original situation and opens up a whole new worldview and brings new understanding. Examples *par excellence* are the parables of the Prodigal Son, the Good Samaritan, the Sower, the Lost Sheep and the Lost Coin. Here Jesus uses the ancient wisdom tradition of storytelling to enable people to experience spiritual understanding where engagement with simple rational debate would not suffice. There is a playful encounter here between the human imagination and the experience of the Holy Spirit spoken through the words of Jesus – the Trinity in action. To begin to appreciate the Trinity, there is something about this re-imagining and wonderment that is needed as a trans-rational discipline, to widen our world-view with the 'trans-possible'.

John's Gospel is packed full of trans-rational meaning, from its poetic opening words to its ending with the promise that when people follow Jesus, they will be invited to encounter the Holy Trinity. The words 'Father, as I am in you and you are in me, so they are in us' are a repeated theme of Jesus' ministry throughout John's Gospel. So trans-rational spiritual knowing finds its fulfilment with the promise that discipleship leads to our adoption and experience of the love of God in everyday life. Prayer becomes a mystical event of joining in with the Trinity, and mission becomes catching up with what the Trinity is already doing. This form of knowing reminds us that we are never truly alone, and that we are all mystically connected to the Divine. Trans-rational wisdom enables us to understand that this ancient doctrine of the Trinity is not just some clever rational human construct, but rather a transcendent gift of love, experienced and handed down to us through the Holy Mothers and Fathers of the Church.

So why is the Trinity so important for trans-rational Christian knowing? Trans-rationalism by itself could be used to argue that all religious traditions and spirituality lead to the same God, the same divine non-human source for all life. This approach diminishes the unique differences of the world's religious traditions and spiritualities. It is the understanding and experience of the Holy Trinity that is unique to Christianity, and makes it a unique revelation of God rather than some form of Jewish cult. Not only this, but it is the implications of the Trinity that help us to find our identity as Christian individuals, as well as to understand the importance of human community. Again, we need to hold in tension the rational and trans-rational mediums of understanding and experiencing the Holy Trinity. Without this, we really do not fully understand the identity, purpose and place of God the Creator, Jesus the Redeemer and Spirit the Counsellor and Comforter.

This all being so, Trinitarian theology and knowing requires us to explore its biblical basis and the experience of the Christian mystics and contemplatives in the East and West, so that we can practise authentic Christianity in terms of worship, mission and community. Holding onto this central concept at the heart of Christian spirituality gives Christians something to say to contemporary society from the heart of authentic faith.

It is the direct experience of the unfathomable love of God that ultimately reveals the truth of God, that leads us to our conversion, and a transformation of our knowing – mind, body and spirit. True knowledge therefore involves both the rational and the trans-rational, and to know the Christian faith fully requires engagement with a trans-rational experience of the Triune God.

2

Experiencing God

On a recent trip with members of the Moot Community to a synagogue in central London, I was reminded that the Christian God
is not that far away from the Jewish one, and that the Christian
formulation of the Trinity emerged out of the experience of a
long faith tradition, one that is shared between Christians, Jews
and Muslims. As I looked through the authorized, revised Jewish
prayer book with which the service was conducted, I was very
moved by a note at the bottom of one of its pages:

> God, the One God has the attributes of Creator, Redeemer and
> Sustainer.

These attributes are the very same three words used in many
Moot Services[1] to express the paradoxically triune nature of the
Christian God. The language is inclusive, and a gender-neutral
alternative to 'Father, Son and Holy Spirit'. What is common to
each of the Abrahamic faiths is the understanding that the nature
of God emerges out of the varied experience of the prophets and
communities of faith in the Hebrew scriptures. In this chapter I
will explore how the experience of God entered the language of
the people of God. I will then draw on the work of a number of
writers to explore ways of understanding and speaking of God that
avoid the mistakes of the past, where God has been conceived of in
overly concrete terms.

---

1 The Moot Community is the Anglican Emerging and Fresh Expression of
church project of which I am the Priest Missioner.

I will draw on the work of Walter Brueggemann to understand how the language used by the Hebrew community to refer to God evolved out of their experience of God as 'event'. I will then explore briefly the circumstances that eventually gave rise to the doctrine of the Trinity, and how these brought about division in the Church. Finally I will consider how the ancient apophatic tradition, often forgotten in the modern church, offers us a renewed approach to understanding God in post-secular times.

It may seem an obvious thing to say, but belief and faith in God did not emerge out of the minds of clever people; rather, they began with people having disorientating and transcendent personal experiences of God. The Hebrew and Christian scriptures are a record of the long and varied history of the experiences people have had of God. They are mostly stories, not theological treatises. At the heart of the Trinitarian mystery is the fact that God, previously unknown, chose to actively engage with human beings, and thereby reveal something of the divine nature. As we will see later, it took some time for Christians to be able to articulate an understanding of God as three-in-one. It took the Early Church Mothers and Fathers around five hundred years to gather together the many hints that pervade scripture and articulate the doctrine of the Trinity. Although the essence of the Trinitarian nature of God is present in the scriptural texts, it must be remembered that the word Trinity itself is nowhere to be found. The Early Church had to wrestle with rational and trans-rational reasoning and experience, about how Jesus the Redeemer, God the Creator and the Holy Spirit all related. Early Church culture was oral rather than word-based, and therefore many of the early understandings of the Christian God evolved out of experience and exploration. We need to remember that the epistles were the very first New Testament sources that the emerging Christian churches had, which helped create the environment for the creation of creeds. So as we seek understanding about the Trinitarian nature of God, we must follow the experiential path through which this revelation was received.

Walter Brueggemann, in his exploration of the texts of the Hebrew scriptures, links language to the self-revelation of God: that is to say that the words and names used of God come directly from the revelatory experience of God.[2] Take for example the word 'to save'. Through the experience of having God provide for their needs, the Hebrew people naturally began to describe God as 'the God who saves'. As time went on, through continued positive experience, the relationship was strengthened and the descriptor was expanded so that God was known as 'the God who saves the people'. A further development results in the title 'the Lord our Saviour'. So with time, people experience the character of God through God's self-revealing activities; the nature of God is experienced, and the language for God develops. It should be noted that the writers of the Hebrew scriptures were wary of using nouns for God. For example, they were careful when using the term 'Saviour'. Brueggemann gives a convincing argument for why this is so. The use of nouns closes down the meaning and naming of God out of experience, and creates a closed or fixed interpretation. Not using nouns avoided the danger of language defining or controlling the experience of God. Instead, relationship with God is on God's terms, respectful of God's fully volitional, self-determining nature. This closing down and controlling of the language used of God was the basic form of idolatry. God becomes a fixed abstraction in the minds of human beings, rather than a thinking, choosing, self-revealing, divine being. The main task of the prophets in the Hebrew scriptures was to prevent this problem by holding nations, their leaders and their priests to account for their idolatrous ways. This ancient problem persists to this day; it is much easier to live with a controllable approximation of God, rather than an active, changing and totally unpredictable God. The people of God are prone to losing their way, or becoming controlling, when this kind of idolatry occurs – but more of

---

2 W. Brueggemann, *Theology of the Old Testament* (Minneapolis: Fortress Press, 1997), pp. 213, 215, 225, 229–30.

that later. For now, we have learned that in the ancient world the experience of the self-revealing activity of God is the means by which we learn who God is, what God is like, and therefore how we name God.

Peter Rollins also rightly challenges the objectification of God through language. Fundamentalism, when it claims to know God fully, is unacceptable for the person of faith, for only God fully knows God. Inherent in the acknowledgement that God self-reveals is the understanding that God also chooses to remain hidden and therefore autonomous over human beings:

> God's revelation is always surrounded by mystery . . . The danger of us thinking we know the truth is idolatry. Paul writes in Colossians 'see to it that no one takes you captive through hollow and deceptive philosophy, which depends on human tradition and the basic principles of this world rather than on Christ.' [In Colossians 2.8] Paul warns us to beware of human abstractions that draw us into a conceptual prison.[3]

Rollins goes further:

> God hides in God's visibility, realizing that revelation embraces concealment at one and the same time as it embraces manifestation and that our various interpretations of revelation will always be provisional, fragile and fragmentary . . . Even the revealed side of God is mysterious.[4]

Scriptural References to the Trinity

With Rollins's insight in mind, what can we safely say about the nature of the Godhead? Can we build a picture that avoids the dangers of abstracting and idolizing our ideas of God? Karl Barth,

---

3 P. Rollins, *How (Not) to Speak of God* (London: SPCK, 2006), pp. 12–16.
4 *Ibid.*, p. 18.

who held dearly the view that scripture is inspired by God through human experience, argued that the Bible itself, with its many hints and comments about the nature of God, actually invites a questioning of that nature.[5] So what are these hints that demand exploration?

For all Muslims, Christians and Jews, experience of God began with Abraham, the root inspiration for all three faiths. God spoke to Abram (as he was originally known), calling him to obedience, to give up everything and leave his own country. Having proved himself faithful to God, a covenant was set up between them. He and his wife Sara both received the letter 'h' in their names as a sign, taken from the name of God, YHWH, of the covenant they had entered into. Muslims cite Ishmael, Abraham's first son, born of Sarah's maidservant Hagar, as the father of their people. Isaac, Abraham's second son, born of Sarah, became the patriarch of the Jews, and Christians also trace the bloodline of Christ back to Isaac and Abraham through the line of David. The 'One God' thoroughly tested Abraham's faith, most notably through the command to sacrifice Isaac, his only son, born to his wife Sarah miraculously late in life. Abraham's faith, stimulated by his testing experiences of God, remained true, and seemed to sustain the faith of those around him. In Genesis 18 he has a transcendent experience of the Divine. The passage describes him becoming aware, through a multi-sensory experience, that the One God was addressing him:

> The Lord appeared to Abraham . . .
> Abraham looked up and saw three men standing nearby. When he saw them, he hurried from the entrance of his tent to meet them and bowed low to the ground. He said, 'If I have found favour in your eyes, my Lord, do not pass your servant by . . . Let me get you something to eat, so you can be refreshed and

---

5 K. Barth, *Church Dogmatics I/I*, as cited in C. Gunton, *Becoming and Being* (London: SCM Press, 2001), p. 127.

then go on your way – now that you have come to your servant.'
'Very well,' they answered, 'do as you say.'

Genesis 18.1–5

From this point on, Abraham's life is transformed as he and his family seek to be obedient to the One God. It marks the beginning of the process whereby YHWH is transformed from being one among many pagan gods, to being Abraham's 'Elohim' – his only God to whom he was committed – and eventually to monotheism, the belief that there is only one God.

This extremely mystical story appears to engage with a God in 'one-ness' yet in three persons. The Lord, the One God appeared in three persons. The story begins with the 'Lord' appearing to Abraham, and then goes on to say it was through the appearance of 'three men'. Abraham then addresses the three figures as 'my Lord', appearing to recognize the figures as an authentic manifestation of God. This encounter is never explained, but in Judaism and Islam the story is interpreted as three angels accompanying the invisible God. Christians, particularly from the Eastern Orthodox tradition, see this story as a key point of the revelation of God's nature. Andrei Rublev's most famous icon depicts the scene in the updated, Trinitarian context of the Christian Eucharist, but more on that later. For now, this event can be seen as the biblical debut, if you like, of the Christian God, 'one-yet-three'. What should be noted is that God is revealed and experienced in a creative and unanticipated event, not as dry abstraction.

In Genesis there are two renderings of the creation story, the second of which gives us an interesting glimpse into the inner life of God. The text speaks symbolically of a multiplicity in the Godhead.

Then God said, 'let US make humankind in OUR own image, according to OUR likeness; and let them steward over the fish of the sea and the birds of the air, over the live stock, over all the earth . . .

Genesis 1.26 [emphasis mine]

It should be noted here that the way Jews and Muslims interpret the Hebrew scriptures is different. Because Christ made direct reference to this passage in the Gospels, it is celebrated as evidence of the eternally pre-existent Trinity. The language is paradoxical, speaking of One-ness, or 'common-unity', for a number of persons. God, conceived of as the One God, is referred to as a plurality.

Jesus, in a spat with the Pharisees, makes reference to Psalm 110. So significant is the reference that all three Synoptic Gospels mention it. The text alludes to an inner life of multiplicity in the Godhead:

> The LORD says to my Lord: Sit at my right hand until I make your enemies a footstall for your feet.
>
> *Psalm 110.1, also in Matthew 22.44,*
> *Mark 12.36, Luke 20.42–43*

There are other Old Testament texts that allude to this 'One God as a community of persons'. Some address the relationship between the person of 'Wisdom' and the 'Creator'. In the book of Proverbs, and the book of Wisdom in the Apocrypha, there is much focus on the idea and identity of a person called 'Wisdom':

> Does not wisdom call,
> and does not understanding raise her voice? . . .
> The Lord created me at the beginning of his work,
> the first of his acts of long ago.
> Ages ago I was set up,
> at the first, before the beginning of the earth.
> When there were no depths I was brought forth,
> when there were no springs abounding with water.
> Before the mountains had been shaped,
> before the hills, I was brought forth –
> when he had not yet made earth and fields,
> or the world's first bits of soil.

When he established the heavens, I was there,
when he drew a circle on the face of the deep,
when he made firm the skies above,
when he established the fountains of the deep,
when he assigned to the sea its limit,
so that the waters might not transgress his command,
when he marked out the foundations of the earth,
then I was beside him, like a master worker;
and I was daily his delight,
rejoicing before him always,
rejoicing in his inhabited world
and delighting in the human race.

Proverbs 8

The text here is highly symbolic, and there is no escaping the identification of the person of Wisdom as a woman. The language here is so dramatic that both Jewish and Christian traditions have toyed with the interpretation that the feminine imagery is more than just a literary device.[6] Clearly Wisdom is credited with nurturing and creative attributes. The identity of the woman was created, not made. She exists before creation, speaks for Yahweh and lives with him (8.22, 9.10). There is a deep intimacy here between the Lord and Wisdom. She is even described as rejoicing in the presence of the Lord (8.30).[7] The encounter is dynamic and playful, and the imagery speaks of participation and co-operation at the creation of the world. The language evokes the imagery of the Genesis creation myths in its use of the symbolism of 'the waters' and 'the deep'. Both Wisdom and Word were present with God before, during and after creation.

In John's Gospel we find the Word present at creation, with many references to the Trinity. It opens with a profound statement about the nature of God:

6 B. Edgar, *The Message of the Trinity* (Leicester: IVP, 2004), p. 87.
7 *Ibid.*, pp. 90–2.

In the beginning was the Word, and the Word was with God, and the Word was God. He was in the beginning with God. All things come into being through him, and without him nothing was made that has been made.

John 1.1–3

The rest of the first chapter makes it clear that the Word refers to Jesus the Christ, and presents us with a paradox: that Jesus 'was with God' and 'was God' at the same time, and that this was so from the beginning of creation. Jesus is also portrayed as the Creator of the whole Universe, so that 'without him nothing was made that has been made'. Further, he frequently refers to the Father as distinct from himself, and also discusses the Holy Spirit as a being distinct from both God the Father, and himself:

'I have said these things to you while I am still with you. But the Advocate, the Holy Spirit, whom the Father will send in my name, will teach you everything, and remind you of all that I have said to you.'

John 14.25–26

So returning to the time of creation, Wisdom is seen as a craftswoman, or the perfecter of creation, while the Word is identified as the one 'through whom all things were made'.[8] So drawing on this connection between Proverbs, Genesis and John 1 we have God the Creator, Wisdom as the Perfecter and the Word through whom all things were made. So God the Creator appears to be dominant at creation, where both the Word and Perfecter are present.

Now the interpretation of these texts has been hotly contested. For some, both the Word and Wisdom have been identified with the person of Christ. Such a view is typical of the Western tradition of thought. Those in the East traditionally make the connection

---

8 *Ibid.*, p. 97.

between the female Wisdom and the person of the Holy Spirit.[9] In the very early Church the word used for the Spirit was expressed in the female, and only later became male.[10] At a later stage I will explore the good reasons why Western theologians may have underestimated the connection between the Spirit and the character of Wisdom, but for now let us hold onto the idea of God participating and co-operating, as having One-ness alongside multiplicity, and as having maternal as well as paternal attributes.

In the first chapter of Luke's Gospel we encounter a connection between differing elements of the Trinity. Take for example God's promise to Mary regarding Jesus:

> The angel said to her, 'The Holy Spirit will come upon you, and the power of the Most High will overshadow you; therefore the child to be born will be holy; he will be called Son of God.'
>
> *Luke 1.35*

In this text, Jesus' conception is understood as a joint effort of both the Holy Spirit and the 'Most High'. If we count the Son taking form in her womb, Mary has a fully Trinitarian experience of God.

In Matthew's gospel in particular, we encounter the three elements of the Trinity as being present at John's baptism of Jesus:

> And when Jesus had been baptized, just as he came up from the water, suddenly the heavens were opened to him, and he saw the Spirit of God descending like a dove and alighting on him.

---

9 K. Norris, *The Cloister Walk* (New York: Riverhead Books, 1987), p. 1; J. Hurtak, *The Holy Spirit: The Feminine Aspect of the Godhead* (Ava, USA: The Academy of Future Science, 2006), accessed 1.11.2011 at http://www.pistissophia.org/The_Holy_Spirit/the_holy_spirit.html.

10 S. G. Hall, *Doctrine and Practice in the Early Church* (London: SPCK, 1991), pp. 41–2, 54–6; J. D. G. Dunn, 'Spirit, Holy Spirit', in D. R. W. Wood (ed.), *New Bible Dictionary Third Edition* (Leicester: IVP, 1996), pp. 1125–9.

And a voice from heaven said, 'This is my Son, the Beloved, whom with I am well pleased.'

Matthew 3.16–17, see also
Mark 1.10–11; Luke 3.22; John 1.32

And again, at the Great Commission, Christ himself talks of God in terms of a plurality of persons:

'Go therefore and make disciples of all nations, baptizing them in the name of the Father and of the Son and of the Holy Spirit, and teaching them to obey everything I have commanded you. And remember, I am with you always, to the end of the age.'

Matthew 28.19–20

In Paul's second letter to the Corinthians we encounter a blessing in the name of the Triune God:

The grace of the Lord Jesus Christ, the love of God, and the communion of the Holy Spirit be with all of you.

2 Corinthians 13.13

Not only does this benediction name the Trinity, it also connects an attribute of God with a particular person of the Trinity. Further to this, the writer has created an order that reflects the experience of the believer: that we experience the grace of Christ through the love of God and are then fully able to participate in the divine life of God through the power of the Holy Spirit. Here we encounter what is called the 'economic Trinity', knowing God through what God has done, through the attributes God has self-revealed.[11]

In Ephesians 1 Paul speaks of his passion for God in terms that are clearly plural. His theology of the Triune Godhead comes out

---

11 Edgar, *Message*, pp. 35–6.

of experience of God through worship. It again emphasizes an order coming out of experience.

> Blessed be the God and Father of our Lord Jesus Christ, who has blessed us in Christ with every spiritual blessing in the heavenly places, just as he chose us in Christ before the foundation of the world to be holy and blameless before him in love. He destined us for adoption as his children through Jesus Christ, according to the good pleasure of his will, to the praise of his glorious grace that he freely bestowed on us in the Beloved. In him we have redemption through his blood, the forgiveness of our trespasses, according to the riches of his grace that he lavished on us. With all wisdom and insight he has made known to us the mystery of his will, according to his good pleasure that he set forth in Christ, as a plan for the fullness of time, to gather up all things in him, things in heaven and things on earth. In Christ we have also obtained an inheritance, having been destined according to the purpose of him who accomplishes all things according to his counsel and will, so that we, who were the first to set our hope on Christ, might live for the praise of his glory. In him you also, when you had heard the word of truth, the gospel of your salvation, and had believed in him, were marked with the seal of the promised Holy Spirit; this is the pledge of our inheritance towards redemption as God's own people, to the praise of his glory.
>
> *Ephesians 1.3–12*

Paul articulates God as a Trinitarian community centred on love: we meet God through Christ, who is blessed by God the Father in the power of the Holy Spirit. Here worship is not merely ritualistic action to please a distant God, but an action through which the believer enters into the life of God. It is a personal relationship to and with God the Father, mediated by Jesus Christ and perfected by the Holy Spirit. This statement articulates how Christian worship is different from the worship of God in the other Abrahamic faiths.

It goes beyond reciting prayers to a transcendent God outside of the here and now, or of intellectual reflection; it is essentially about invitation to join in the community of the Godhead in the here and now, and be transformed through such an ongoing experience.

In Christianity, worship and encountering the Trinity in the here and now go together.[12] So it is with this Trinitarian idea that we understand that much of discipleship is centred around a God who is both transcendent and immanent, where God is present in the world, engaging in the world, so that the Christian life is about catching up with what God is already doing.

In the letter to the Hebrews, we begin to hear early formulations for the atonement, or 'at-one-ment', which is about attempting to understand how Christ through the Trinity brings reconciliation between God and humanity for sin:

> How much more, then, will the blood of Christ, who through the eternal Spirit offered himself unblemished to God, cleanse our consciences from acts that lead to death, so that we may serve the living God!
>
> *Hebrews 9.14* (NIV)

Here the Trinitarian formulation is used to cast a vision of transformation. Through the crucifixion, death and resurrection of Christ, and the power of the Holy Spirit, we as followers of Christ are enabled to be free from the consequences and distortions of our own selfishness and self-preoccupation (which the Christian tradition calls 'sin'), through an ongoing and living relationship with the Trinity.

In the first letter of John we find a very strong statement of the co-existing reality of three persons in the one Godhead:

> For there are three that bear record in heaven, the Father, the Word, and the Holy Ghost: and these three are one. And there

---

12 *Ibid.*, pp. 53–5.

are three that bear witness in earth, the Spirit, and the water, and the blood: and these three agree in one.

1 John 5.7–8[13] (KJB)

The selections of texts we have explored in this section really help us to see the biblical inspiration for the Trinity, and how its formulation, under the circumstances, was quite natural.

One of the most challenging circumstances for the Early Church was the contestation over the nature of the Godhead, where the use of scripture itself was no guarantee of orthodoxy. One of the first heretics, Arius, made appeal to scripture for the support of his idea that Jesus was not fully human. The Church continued to wrestle with the biblically revealed nature of God for the first five hundred years of its existence. In what are now known as the Ecumenical Councils, it met to attempt to bring some coherence to the faith. Some of today's more radically minded Christians see these councils as ending the important role that experience had played in knowing God; however, there is clearly a difference between seeking to paint a coherent picture of the nature of God that takes into consideration the entire, varied biblical revelation, and an outright idolatrous objectification that leaves no room whatever for the role of experience. Some believed that Jesus wasn't really human; others that Jesus wasn't really God; and others still that there was only One God and that Jesus and the Holy Spirit were not God, but merely close relatives. Others believed that Jesus and the Father were related, but not the Holy Spirit. Many were greatly influenced by Greek and Eastern philosophy, which sometimes brought illumination to understanding, but at other times distortion. The Early Church Mothers and Fathers had to explore the fragments and hints about Jesus and the Trinity to understand what God had revealed.

---

13 There is much debate surrounding this particular text, as many scholars are convinced that it was added to scripture long after the original was written, and was influenced by a more developed Trinitarian theology.

The Influence of the Cappadocian Mothers and Fathers of the Early Church

Cappadocia, located in modern-day Turkey, was an influential Roman province. It became the stage for a number of highly influential theologians. St Macrina was the grandmother and influence to a number of highly important Early Church Mothers and Fathers. These included, among others, Macrina the Younger (327–379), Basil the Great (329–379), Naukratios the Anchorite (330–357), Gregory of Nyssa (340–394) and their great friend Gregory of Nazianzus (329–379).[14] Together they have become known as the Cappadocian Mothers and Fathers.[15] The letters and theological writings between these family members and friends, particularly those of Basil and the Gregories,[16] have been retained by the Church. It is these discussions and explorations that led to the conceptualization of the Trinity in the Early Church, articulating a theology that emphasized the distinctiveness of each of the three persons of God.[17] St Macrina exerted a huge influence upon their thinking. A disciple of Origen had tutored her, and it was her theological education that provided the foundation for her grandchildren's work. They took it further by utilizing the metaphor of image to explain the divine nature of Christ, and to say that the Father and the Son are equal in all things, including being and eternity.[18] God as image is made reference to in the scriptures, where it says of Christ:

He is the image of the invisible God, the firstborn of all creation.

Colossians 1.15

---

14 G. A. Barrois (ed.), *The Fathers Speak* (New York: SVP, 1986), pp. 26–30; A. Meredith SJ (ed.), Gordon S. Wakefield, *A Dictionary of Christian Spirituality* (London: SCM Press, 1983), pp. 68–70.

15 *Ibid.*

16 *Ibid.*, pp. 15–219.

17 Hall, *Doctrine*, p. 156.

18 *Ibid.*

Rather than closing down meaning and creating certainty, the Cappadocians believed that it was impossible to fully understand the nature of God, and challenged those who proposed such ideas in the early councils. To quote Basil: 'We know the greatness of God, his power, his goodness, his providence over us, and the justice of his judgement, but not his very essence . . . we know our God from his operations, but do not undertake to approach near his essence.'[19]

Apophatic approach

A focus on knowing God through individual experience, where God is never fully knowable and where descriptive language can never totally define God.

Platonic thought

Thinking derived from the Greek philosopher Plato. The main tenet of his thought was that the highest level of knowledge is around goodness, and the call to live virtuously. This good is related to justice and beauty. Human beings can learn of this good through encounter with the Divine, where God is to be experienced as an event.

The Cappadocians were responsible for promoting an apophatic approach to experiencing and understanding the Divine, infused with the insights of Platonic thought that denied that God's being can be absolutely known or defined. Instead it focuses on the varied and often paradoxical information revealed by God in scripture.

---

19 *Ibid.*, pp. 157–8.

So the Cappadocians argued that God has a general or common essence (*ousia*) and that there are three persons (*prosopa*) each existing as concrete individuals with their own identities (*hypostasis*). In nature and being the three are absolutely the same, coeternal and infinite, and utterly distinct from creation, which is finite and exists within time. But they are distinguished from each other by the characteristics of each: the Father is distinguished as the Cause, the Son by being the only begotten, the Spirit by proceeding from the Father. At the time, the Cappadocians went further than others had before them, by identifying the Holy Spirit as a person of the Trinity of the same substance and importance as the Father and the Son.[20]

The Cappadocian Trinitarian formulations maintained that despite God's self-revelations, God remains somewhat mysteriously concealed. It further affirmed that God, in God's being, was not static, but something fluid, vibrant and creative.

The Implications of Perichoresis

Perhaps the greatest gift of the Cappadocians to the Church was the concept of perichoresis, which was formulated by them and developed by St John of Damascus. It draws on two Greek words that do not translate easily into English. 'Peri' has a meaning close to the words connecting, surrounding, enclosing, relating in close proximity, with the sense of being alive and dynamic.[21] 'Choresis' has a meaning close to being distinguishable parts making up something as a whole; the separation of something into two or more parts.[22] Put these two words together, and we have a strong

---

20 *Ibid.*, p. 158.
21 A. E. Laurita, *Greek Roots and Their Modern English Spellings: A Dictionary of Roots Transliterated from Ancient Greek with Their Modern English Spellings* (New York: Leonardo Press, 1989).
22 *Ibid.*

metaphor of something in its 'one-ness' being expressed in dynamic separate parts.

Utilizing this concept of perichoresis theologically, it describes the Trinity as three substances, three persons who dwell in one another.[23] 'Peri' creates the sense of dynamism and activity. Here the Creator, Redeemer and Sustainer are interpenetrative, embracing and permeating each other.[24]

This dynamic or fluid understanding of the nature of God has its basis in John's Gospel, where it says that 'the Father is in the Son and Son is in the Father'.[25] This indwelling expresses and realizes a profound sense of fellowship between the persons of the Trinity. The perichoretic relationship is not hierarchical or authoritarian; rather it is characterized by unity in diversity, perfect love, justice and interdependency. It describes a God centred in mystery; a God who is both transcendent (outside of here and now) yet mysteriously immanent (actually here and now). But at the same time, it names a God who only partially reveals the nature of God, through God's actions. No one has ever fully seen God. This understanding does not sell out to certainty, but encourages a sense of a complex and apophatic God, a God slightly out of reach whom we will never fully know.

So we meet a God through an apophatic vision of faith and an experience of God's action in human lives – or what has become called (un) knowing: knowing God through mystical encounter rather than knowing God as a set of objectified facts.

In the tradition of the Eastern Church, perichoresis is seen as a dynamic dance in which the different persons of the Trinity lead at different stages in salvation history. The very nature of God is centred on creativity, love and intimacy; a creativity that led to the pouring out of a divine love that created the whole cosmos. All matter, both animate and inanimate, was therefore created out of

23 A. Walker, *God of the Christians: The Spirit and the Trinity* (London: HTB Bookshop, 2007), ref. 6374, 6375, 6376.
24 Gunton, *Becoming*, p. 232.
25 Walker, *Christians*, ref. 6374–6.

27

the expression of love internally generated within the Trinity, and expressed out into the infinity of space and time. So the whole of creation has come out of the inner worship and creativity of God.

John Zizioulas reminds us that this perichoretic understanding of God is that of a being in communion or common-unity.[26] God is seen to model profound devotion to God-self. In Rublev's icon of the Trinity, it is no coincidence that the three figures are engaged in the celebration of the Eucharist. The image perfectly reflects the qualities of perichoresis I have outlined above, and as such the icon has become very important to many Emerging and Fresh Expressions of church. It is interesting that this understanding of the Trinity has been so neglected in the Western Church, particularly within the Reformed stream of theology. To understand more about how we have arrived at this situation, and its significance, we must go back to church history and the Ecumenical Councils.

Doctrines and Division

The first three Ecumenical Councils in the Early Church were very important for the Christian faith. The first, at Nicea (325 CE), addressed a coherent understanding of the significance of Jesus Christ. The second, at Constantinople (381 CE), addressed a full understanding of the Trinity, which radically included the Holy Spirit as God. The third and final, the Council of Chalcedon (451 CE), affirmed the authenticity of the findings of the two earlier councils, and further strengthened an understanding of Jesus as fully God and fully human.[27] As was stated earlier, much of the debate was concerned with establishing consistency in the interpretation of scripture. Many of the heresies that the Church had battled with were extremely mystical, which might explain why it took the Church so long to be able to acknowledge the Holy Spirit as God. In fact, as Professor Andrew Walker has said, the doctrine

---

26 Gunton, *Becoming*, p. 232.
27 Walker, *Christians*, ref. 6375.

of the Trinity appears to downplay the Holy Spirit somewhat,[28] and could even be criticized as understating the significance of the person of the Holy Spirit. This may have occurred for fear of promoting heresies, which up until the formulation of this doctrine had emphasized the divine nature of Jesus over his humanity. So we are left with a strong sense of the identities of the Creator and the Redeemer, and a somewhat faceless Holy Spirit. However, the doctrine did establish a fresh understanding of the Trinity. The English translation approximates to:

The Creed	*The Attributes*
We believe in one God,	
the Father, the Almighty,	*The Father*
maker of heaven and earth,	*The Creator*
of all that is, seen and unseen.	
We believe in one Lord, Jesus Christ,	
the only Son of God,	
eternally begotten of the Father,	*The Son*
God from God, light from light,	*Fully God*
true God from true God,	*Fully Human*
begotten, not made,	*The Redeemer*
of one Being with the Father;	
through him all things were made.	
For us and for our salvation	
he came down from heaven,	
was incarnate of the Holy Spirit	
and the Virgin Mary	
and became truly human.	*Fully Human*
For our sake he was crucified under	
Pontius Pilate;	
he suffered death and was buried.	
On the third day he rose again	

---

28 *Ibid.*

in accordance with the Scriptures;
he ascended into heaven
and is seated at the right hand of
the Father.   *Fully God*
He will come again in glory to judge the
living and the dead,
and his kingdom will have no end.

We believe in the Holy Spirit, the Lord,
the giver of life,   *The Holy Sprit*
who proceeds from the Father,   *The Sustainer*
who with the Father and the Son is
worshiped and glorified,
who has spoken through the prophets.
We believe in one holy catholic and
    apostolic Church.
We acknowledge one baptism for the
    forgiveness of sins.
We look for the resurrection of the dead,
and the life of the world to come. Amen.[29]

This creed should sound very familiar, as it is recited regularly in many church traditions as an act of faith. Its doctrines remain widely accepted by the majority of churches in the East and the West, including the Reformed churches; both Luther and Calvin fully accepted the Nicene Creed.[30] However, it was not plain sailing in the East. A number of churches, including the Ethiopian and Coptic Orthodox churches, and the Monophysite churches, dissented. This resulted in the first great division in the Early Church. In the face of significant political pressure, these texts, which were the gift of an ongoing tradition of experience-led revelation of God, became dogma or, put another way, became objectified. We must

29 Walker, *Christians,* ref. 6375.
30 *Ibid.*

remember that all words we use to understand God are provisional, never definitive, as God can never be fully explained. All revelation of God to humanity is necessarily mediated through human understanding and is therefore subjective. The Nicene Creed, although widely and historically accepted, must be understood as an imperfect human construct. For example, as we will see later, it says very little about the actual life and ministry of the Redeemer. We must be attentive to the Cappadocian Mothers and Fathers who firmly believed that God could never be rendered fully knowable. We must always honour God's autonomy over all of our ideas about God.

St Augustine's Interpretation

Not getting off lightly either, the Western Church was also to experience its share of division. Augustine of Hippo (354–430 CE), arguably the Father of Western Christianity, put forward an interpretation of the Trinity that has caused complication and dispute ever since.[31] His work was undertaken using a Latin translation of the original Greek text of the Nicene Creed, and he understood God as *one substance in three persons*.[32] Unfortunately, the translation did not carry quite the same nuance as the original text, and Augustine made the mistake of conceiving of the Trinity as a set of relationships rather than unique personalities or particularities.[33] And therefore he said: 'When it is asked, "Three what?", human speech labours under great difficulty. Nevertheless "Three persons" has been said, not in order to say just that, but to avoid saying nothing.'[34] His Trinitarianism lacks the perichoretic dimension intended by the Cappadocians, and therefore God became seen in much more static terms. Many see this as a distinct weakness of Western theology, and as an aggravation of the

---

31 Hall, *Doctrine*, p. 159.
32 *Ibid.*, p. 201.
33 Walker, *Christians*, ref. 6375.
34 Hall, *Doctrine*, p. 201.

tension between the East and West. Unfortunately Augustine took this further with the inclusion of the *filioque* clause, added in the West to the Nicene Creed.

He claimed, as others had before him, that the Holy Spirit proceeds from the Father '*and the Son*'. This was not in the original Nicene Creed, and it portrayed the Holy Spirit as subservient to the Son. He failed to see the Holy Spirit as a full person, and therefore as not equal to the Father and the Son. Photius (*c.* 820–893 CE) talked of this as a 'downgrading' of the Holy Spirit, which made the Spirit more of a receiver than an equal person.[35] Colin Gunton (1941–2003) has argued that this downplaying of the person of the Holy Spirit has created a weakness peculiar to Western theology.

The *filioque* clause was incorporated into the Nicene Creed in the Western Church, in response to a resurgence of Arianism in the eighth century. The decision was taken at a Church Council in Toledo, and the revised Creed, which was to become the default option for Western churches, was used by the Bishop of Rome at a Church service in Rome. This caused a huge row, as no Ecumenical Council had ever agreed to it, which eventually led to the split between the Western and Eastern Churches. It should be noted that there is no biblical justification for the *filioque* clause, and it is counter to a perichoretic understanding of God. We are left with a distorted vision of the Trinity in the Western Church, which has remained, as Professor Andrew Walker has stated many times, the Achilles heel of Western Christianity.[36]

The Contribution of Karl Barth

Karl Barth (1886–1968) challenged this static and objectified understanding of the Trinity in the West. He reconnected the

---

35 Walker, *Christians*, ref. 6375.
36 *Ibid*, ref. 6375.

doctrine of the Trinity to a theology of God's self-revelation.[37] In so doing he reinstated a dynamic, perichoretic understanding of God, where God is an event, a happening.[38] God's nature as Father, Son and Spirit is identical to God's nature as Revealer, Revelation and Revealing. And it is in this multiplicity that God's unity consists. Barth states:

> If revelation is to be taken seriously as God's presence . . . then in no sense can Christ and the Spirit be subordinate hypostases . . . revelation and revealing must be equal to the revealer.[39]

Under the cloak of modern language, Barth reconnects us with the dynamic God of the Cappadocians. He talks about the being of God as the 'becoming of God',[40] and as such God is understood not as a transcendent thing but as a transcendent happening.[41] God is not eternalized in the past, but seen as the Lord of the future.[42] This is a God of relationships, of three equal persons.[43]

While Barth's approach to the Trinity does challenge Augustine's 'depersonalization' of the Holy Spirit, Gunton holds that the significance of the Holy Spirit remains understated, albeit less so than in Augustine's writing.[44]

This weakness of the person of the Holy Spirit in Western theology, coupled with an overemphasis on the Father and the Son, has led to real problems for the Western Church, to which we must now return.

---

37 Edgar, *Message*, pp. 90–7.

38 Gunton, *Becoming*, p. 140.

39 K. Barth, *Church Dogmatics I/I*, as cited in Gunton, *Becoming*, p. 139.

40 Gunton, *Becoming*, p. 138.

41 *Ibid.*, p. 140.

42 R. W. Jenson, *God After God A Study in the Theology of Karl Barth* (New York: NY Press, 1963), pp. 76, 96 as cited in Gunton, *Becoming*, p. 140.

43 Gunton, *Becoming*, pp. 143–4, 229.

44 *Ibid.*, pp. 163–6, 233–40.

GOD UNKNOWN

Faith as Desire and How (Not) to Speak of God

The Western Church has long been guilty of an overemphasis on orthodoxy, or right thinking, to the detriment of orthopraxy, or right action. Too much significance has been placed on objective truth, which, some have argued, distorts faith. I turn to Peter Rollins again:

> God is not a theoretical problem to somehow resolve, but rather a mystery to be participated in . . . Religious truth is that which transforms reality rather than that which describes it . . . God is not the object of our thoughts but rather the absolute subject before whom we are the object. This is confirmed in baptism when we say that we are 'baptized in the name of the Father, Son and Holy Ghost'. Here we do not name God but God's name names us.[45]

As a Christian of the Western tradition, I have much experience of the reductive drive to fully know God, of the desire for certainty that distorts faith. The Emerging Church, and I would argue the Deep Church movement, recognize the importance of a deeply held Trinitarian theology that counters the superficial drive for an objective certainty that boxes God in. Both movements seek a re-awakening of the Christian faith as an orientation of the heart, following the unpredictable, dynamic movements of a God who will always elude our desire for control. It is my belief that this ancient:future faith can relate profoundly to a post-secular culture. It challenges us to seek God in the mystery of transcendence, rather than in objectification, to discern God through the experiences of a life of worship that joins in with what God is doing. This apophatic form of faith seeks understanding, but not certainty, and is happy that we will never fully know God. This is a mature form of faith.

---

45 Rollins, *How*, pp. 22–3.

When we read that Christ is the truth and that knowing the truth will set us free, we come face to face with truth, not as the objective affirmation of a proposition, but rather as that which arises from a life-giving encounter. The truth of Christianity is not described, it is experienced.[46]

This form of faith has much to do with the idea of becoming. First, we encounter in the scriptures a God who over time begins to self-reveal the divine nature in relationship to human beings. Beginning with Abraham, God 'becomes' in human experience as a transcendent event. Over the course of history people began to articulate their becoming experience of God, which ultimately climaxed in the Nicene Creed and an understanding of the Triune God. Further, as this God addresses particular human beings, encouraging transcendent spiritual experience, people form expressions of faith arising out of these encounters. Life then becomes a process of human becoming out of this dynamic form of faith. By implication Christ, the image of the invisible God, comes into human history instituting a Christian faith and an emerging form of church. After Christ, the Spirit as the Counsellor, Sustainer, Companion and Perfecter constitutes an emerging form of church that grows out of the community of the disciples. Faith comes out of individual experience of the Triune God, and the Church itself is challenged to model itself on the very nature of the 'becoming of God'.

Reflection

The decline experienced by the Western Church throughout the period of modernity and now in post-secularization is due in the main to an inadequate theism. Conceptions of God as one's *best friend*, or as excessively immanent or transcendent, are the result

---

46 *Ibid.*, p. 56.

of a failure to accept the validity of, and move beyond, the critique of the Enlightenment emancipators. These are still commonly held views, but they do not provide a form of faith that can withstand the cultural and intellectual climate of our times. It is my belief that a Trinitarian conception of the nature of God is well suited to the challenge we face in seeking to reconnect people with deep spiritual meaning. In an age when so many are turned off church by what they perceive as over-simplification, we downplay the nature of God at our peril.

3

Divine Open-endedness

The penny dropped for me in 1990, in Leeds, in the very early hours of one Sunday morning, at a club night called *Devotions*. I had come along interested to know what this 'dance night with a spiritual kick' was all about. For the previous few years I had had a growing sense of attraction towards spiritual stuff in general, and Christianity in particular. It had all started with nothing more significant than a gut feeling that, somewhere out there, was a loving, transcendent force that was on my side. The feeling grew through moving experiences at Easter and Christmas church services, and a tearful viewing of *Jesus Christ Superstar* on television. Unsurprisingly, given that I had come from an un-churched, un-believing context, I found that I never quite fitted in at traditional churches. I nevertheless continued to heed the cosmic force that seemed to be beckoning me to come closer. The club night in Leeds was something of a eureka moment. A 'gospel garage' track came blasting out of the speakers, with words about the Three in One God, and of redemptive love, and I was struck by just how full of hope it was. Images were projected on screens depicting the Trinity dancing together, beckoning the onlookers to join in and have a good time. I realized there and then that I was in the awesome presence of a God who accepted and loved me, and that that nightclub had become church to me, a place of worship. God wasn't bound by four old stone walls, nor was church. It could be relevant, fun and participative. The event was put on by the alternative worship group called 'Warehouse', now 'Visions', based at

St Michael-Le-Belfry in York. The club in Leeds liked them because their djing and vjing were often better than their secular peers. I went on to be involved in the life of the Warehouse community, irresistibly drawn by the transcendent sense of God's presence I encountered there. In whatever they did there was always a strong sense of the person of the Holy Spirit being present, aside from just God the Father and the Son, a characteristic I had not really encountered before.

When I had become a Christian at the age of seventeen, two years before the club night in Leeds, my understanding of God's nature was limited to the deity of Christ. Lip service had been given to the other members of the Godhead, but by comparison with the person of Christ they seemed wholly inadequate. The Father seemed like an old, vengeful man, mostly relegated to ancient history, and the Spirit something of an impersonal enigma, who seemed to operate like the engine of God. The main message I seemed to be getting was that, as the song says, 'it's all about you, all about you, Jesus'. Curiously, in the months following my baptism many of those who were baptized with me began to disappear from the local church scene. I remember asking one of my newly de-churched friends how this had happened. I'll never forget what he said: 'Well my life got complicated, rough stuff happened, and kept happening. So I began to ask, if Jesus is my friend, why is this happening? I came to believe that Jesus was not my friend at all, as he didn't show it. Jesus gave up on me, so I gave up on Jesus.' This is an all too familiar story, and I have heard it repeated in different forms all over Britain. We suffer from a very poor understanding of the nature of God, which is unable to sustain us in difficult times. As we explored in the last chapter, the Western Church from Augustine onwards has had a weakened understanding of the Trinity, and in particular the Holy Spirit, and this has impoverished generation after generation of Christians.

In my own experience, the person of the Holy Spirit was often merged with the person of Christ. There was widespread ignorance concerning the dependence of Jesus on the work of the Holy Spirit, visible throughout the Gospels. Instead the Holy Spirit was watered down to little more than the impersonal engine of God, or the formless wind of God. Walker and Bretherton explain the situation well:

> The story of redemption can be told as a tale of Father and Son in which the Holy Spirit is neither here nor there. The Spirit can also be expelled from the Godhead through reductionist theologizing: even in Pentecostal circles he is sometimes depicted as a 'force field' that emanates from Jesus. The Holy Ghost it would seem is welcomed as power but far less as person.[1]

In many churches, the Spirit seems to act like a magic force that can be invoked in order to stir congregations up into an ecstatic frenzy. Admittedly, the Holy Spirit does seem to manifest in somewhat unpredictable ways at times, but there is a high price to pay for an impersonal, 'magical force' view of the Holy Spirit, and the correlating hierarchical view of God's nature that results. For example, there is often a strong sense of fear of secular culture, resulting from the belief that the world is utterly fallen, evil and godless. Preparation for mission activities in the 'outside world' often involves 'praying on' the spiritual armour of God for protection in a society where the same God is otherwise absent. The truth is that this perichoretic God is fully involved in the world. Looking back at my personal experiences of such churches, I can see how this entire thinking is based on a profoundly limited understanding of the person of the Holy Spirit. We were aggressive, seeking to argue people into the Kingdom

---

1 L. Bretherton and A. Walker, *Recovering Deep Church in Remembering Our Future* (London: Paternoster, 2007), p. 13.

by rational debate, and we had little appreciation for the love of God that was already at work in the world, seeking to restore all things into right relationship. I look back with sadness about how little I knew and how badly I had been taught about the nature of God.

In the previous chapters we saw how worship can become mechanical when it is not seen in the personal, perichoretic context of the Trinity. The same is true with prayer, which in many churches is described as little more than telling God what's on your mind. The Holy Spirit fulfils the function of passing on our spiritual shopping list to God the Father. I have heard it preached from the pulpit that the contemplative forms of prayer are an indulgence, a view I am now completely at odds with. This view demonstrates a profound under-appreciation of the perichoretic nature of the Trinitarian God. Prayer, like worship, is about encountering and relating with the Triune God as an expression of the desires of one's heart. In many churches, intercessory prayer begins with the phrase 'in the power of the Spirit and in union with Christ, let us pray to the Father'. A personal view of the Holy Spirit necessitates a degree of relational maturity on our part, so that prayer comes to involve listening as much as it does talking, giving as much as taking. Contemplative forms of prayer, rather than being an indulgence, are in my view the medium of maturity in prayer and intercession.

Prayer should not be exercised as a power that we have over God, as if God were a heavenly servant at our beck and call; quite the opposite. It is about us learning to be in relationship with and through the Divine, a relationship full of mystery and encounter. Nor should it be characterized by the mechanical placation of an angry God, but by grace, love and intimacy. Through prayer we can learn to love as God loves, in powerlessness and humility, and so gain the most profound sense of inner peace. It is through this relational, 'I–thou' approach, that we are enabled to become fully human, going deeper into God and discovering ever more about who we really are.

The 'I–Thou' relationship

Martin Buber, a twentieth-century writer, used two pairs of words to describe two fundamentally different types of human relationship: 'I–It' and 'I–Thou'. Our human individual identity ultimately relates to God as Thou. In the I–Thou relation there are no barriers, and this means that every human being can relate directly to God. God is ever-present in human consciousness. People derive their identity, consciously or not, from their relationship to God the divine Thou.

Worship as Temple Appeasement

The temple was for many years the geographical centre of the Jewish faith. It was the place where, through the service of the High Priest, atonement (at-one-ment) was made for the sins of the people. Christians have historically understood that Christ replaced the High Priest, and that he personally atoned for our sin, so that through the power of the Holy Spirit we may find peace with God. A full treatment of the controversies surrounding the various atonement theories is beyond the scope of this book, but what I would like to comment on is the generally accepted notion that Christ has liberated us from the requirement to practise temple worship. What has in effect happened is that the idea of temple worship has been reconstituted in the light of Christ's atonement. The New Testament espouses the view that each Christian has become a 'temple of the Holy Spirit',[2] which means that individuals have direct access to God through relationship with Christ. It also emphasizes the communal aspect of relationship with God: 'when two or more are gathered, I will be there also'.[3] Christian

---

2 1 Corinthians 3.16, 6.19; 2 Corinthians 6.16.
3 Matthew 18.20.

worship then is ultimately about our relationship with God and each other, in what the Apostle Paul calls 'the body of Christ'.[4] The highest form of this worship is expressed in Holy Communion or Eucharist, where God is made present mystically through the sacrament to those gathered together. Here worship is the gift of participation through the Holy Spirit in the Son's communion with the Father. Trinitarian worship is about God coming to us and lifting us up.[5] Worship therefore centred on God not only the object of worship, but also the one who leads and inspires the worship.

Unfortunately for some, worship in church has come to bear a distinct resemblance to temple worship. Instead of celebrating and encountering the goodness of God, people gather in order to appease the anger of God. Christ has become the warrior-king God of the Hebrew scriptures, and is no longer an image of powerlessness, love and grace, but of dominance, wrath and judgement. Worship is something done before God rather than to and with God, a work rather than a gift of grace.[6] The emphasis tends not to be on the grace and compassion of God, but on sinfulness and the need for repentance. The resulting guilt that many people experience is used to clobber them into conformity with the ruling moral norms. Such churches tend to have a weakened understanding of the Trinity, and a belief that God has been rendered fully knowable by revelation. This concept of God is essentially expressing a Unitarian theology, which is, practically speaking, anti-Trinitarian. Many of these forms of church also believe strongly in what has been called the 'penal substitution' atonement theory. Here the Father or Creator God is seen to be fermentingly angry because of human sin. Jesus therefore had to die to appease the Father and so to pacify God's anger. Opinion is divided in the Christian Church, but I am most definitely in the camp that find

---

4 1 Corinthians 12.27; Ephesians 4.12.
5 B. Edgar, *The Message of the Trinity*, (Leicester: IVP, 2004) p. 23.
6 *Ibid.*, pp. 22–3.

this theory deeply disturbing, and inconsistent with Trinitarian thinking and the very words of Christ in the New Testament. In *Threshold to the Future*, Mike Riddell emphasizes that such churches seem to have reverted to non-Trinitarian monotheism, where the significance of the Trinity as a loving, creative divinity is somewhat lost. Such churches tend to have a strict, if unspoken, moral code, and an ungenerous attitude towards human nature, which Riddell calls the 'sin of Holiness'.[7] When we read about Jesus getting angry in the Gospels, it is mostly directed at the Scribes and Pharisees. He came down very heavily on them for the absolutizing tendency of their faith, which was often dehumanizing, oppressive and judgemental.[8] Christ challenges us to live instead by the law of love, which is a reflection of the self-giving deference modelled in the Trinity. Holding onto the mystery of the God we see there restrains our oft-felt desire to resolve all mysteries. The result is always a more inclusive, humane expression of faith.[9]

As I noted earlier, many have failed to recognize Christ's dependency upon the Holy Spirit, seen throughout the Gospels, for the many miracles he performed.[10] While preaching about his own ministry at the synagogue in Nazareth, Christ quoted from the prophecies of Isaiah to highlight the partnership he had with the Holy Spirit:

'The Spirit of the Lord is upon me, because he has anointed me to bring good news to the poor. He has sent me to proclaim release to the captives and recovery of sight to the blind, to let the oppressed go free, to proclaim the year of the Lord's favour.'[11]

Luke 4.18–19, Isaiah 61.1–2

---

7 M. Riddell, *Threshold to the Future* (London: SPCK, 1998), pp. 72–87.

8 Riddell, *Threshold*, pp. 72–7.

9 J. Caputo, *On Religion*, Thinking in Action Series (London: Routledge, 2001), pp. 92–3, 108.

10 Matthew 12.23–33; Mark 2.8; Luke 4.14–19.

11 Luke 4.18–19; Isaiah 61.1–2.

Much Western theological writing has under-appreciated this partnership, and lost a sense of the personhood of the Spirit. Ramsey and Terwilliger have challenged this, and proffer the Eastern Orthodox notion of the 'Christ of the Spirit' as an alternative to the Western emphasis on the 'Spirit of Christ'.[12] Here, the life of Jesus Christ is seen as the greatest work of the Holy Spirit:

> He is incarnate by the Spirit, commissioned at his baptism by the Spirit, driven into the wilderness by the Spirit, empowered in his mighty works by the Spirit and raised from death by the Spirit.[13]

Seeing the Holy Spirit as a subservient, inferior member of the Godhead results in a divine, exclusively male, 'one-parent family'. This renders God very susceptible to manipulation by, and as a justification for, oppressive patriarchal ideologies. The Spirit contributes many attributes commonly thought of as female, and therefore serves to de-gender God. If we begin to see the life of Christ, his wisdom and miracles as the result of co-operation with the person of the Holy Spirit, it opens the way for us to see more clearly the depth of the Trinitarian presence of God in scripture. The Spirit is no longer the dynamo or the faceless power of God, but a person of equal stature to the Creator and the Redeemer. We then begin to see that Christ's very ministry modelled participation in the Godhead. This brings real meaning to Christ's call for his followers to join with the Holy Spirit, which he was to send after his ascension. The Church Mothers, Fathers and mystics talk about how the work of prayer involves listening, discernment, and then joining in with what God is already doing. If we are truly attentive to the Gospels, we will not see Jesus himself as the end or goal of our faith. On the contrary, the Redeemer always points

---

12 M. Ramsey, R. E. Terwilliger and A. M. Allchin, *The Charismatic Christ* (London: DLT, 1974), p. 7.

13 *Ibid.*, pp. 6, 28–9.

beyond himself, into the mystery of the Trinity,[14] where the true focus of our worship should be set.[15]

One of the implicit strengths of Trinitarian theology is that God is seen to model unity in diversity. Of course this is largely lost in Western thinking, with its overemphasis on the Father and Son. As a result, much of Western church history can be said to reflect a drive for 'unity in conformity', which has led to some of the worst atrocities and divisions the world has seen. Jesus Christ commanded us to strive for the highest form of unity, that of the love of brothers and sisters, so that people would know that he is God.[16] Unfortunately, it seems that the main concern in the West has been orthodoxy rather than orthopraxy. We therefore have a history deeply marked by schism and disunity, where reform was often undertaken in a divisive spirit, which put right belief before unity. And this is obviously still the case for many Christians. Jane Williams, the wife of the present Archbishop of Canterbury, demonstrated this very well in a lecture she gave recently, at St Paul's Theological Centre in London. She took a Bible, and said to those gathered, 'Here I have a Bible. What would you feel like if I start tearing out pages?' The class looked on horrified, and some responded with cries of 'You can't, that's terrible!' Jane continued, 'So you feel very strongly when I tear out pages of this Bible, a book I can buy a replacement for anywhere? How come we find it so easy to neglect and break relationships with other Christians, that once broken, are almost impossible to repair?' Her delivery was passionate and carried the weight of the conviction she had. The class fell silent, as the uncomfortable truth of what she said sunk in. So often we have put ideas of orthodoxy before our love for one another. In the face of the struggles facing the Anglican Communion at present, it is clear she still hopes for 'unity in diversity'.

---

14 Ramsey *et al.*, *Charismatic Christ*, p. 24.
15 *Ibid.*, p. 25.
16 John 13.34–35.

One of the questions I continue to reflect on is whether the Reformation happened in the West because of a poor understanding of the Holy Spirit, with an emphasis on 'truth' and 'freedom' rather than the 'unity' that seemed to matter so much to Christ. A short story will illustrate my point. I went on a short break late last year to stay with a friend in Northern Ireland. On one occasion, while visiting a small scenic town outside Belfast, I was struck by how many churches could be found on the high street. The Anglican Church of Ireland was a short distance from the slightly younger First Presbyterian Church. A few yards up the road from this, beyond the Second Presbyterian Church, was the actual Reformed Presbyterian Church. At the end of the road was the local charismatic evangelical church. Being such a small town, it was a very sad, very graphic portrayal of the relentless force of reform, and the way in which unity has been taken so lightly.

I have little evidence here to support my hypothesis, but I would guess that the aforementioned weakness in Western theology was a significant factor in the precipitation of the Reformation. I also wonder whether the tendency towards institutionalization in the Western Church is due in part to the lack of a vision of renewal, born out of an understanding of the person of the Holy Spirit. It is fascinating that there has not been anything like the same number of reformation movements in the Eastern Church as in the West. This may be due to the relative political instability in the East: church leaders were never as powerful as those in the West. Nevertheless, I would suggest that the appreciation of the perichoresis of God, and the importance of the Holy Spirit in their theology, has helped them maintain the unity demanded by Christ. I believe that Emerging and Fresh Expressions of church are rediscovering this understanding, and the space that it opens up for unity in diversity in the twenty-first century. It is part of a growing discontent for certain elements of our Western theological inheritance, and an appreciation for certain elements of the East. I also believe that the charismatic renewal of the 1960s and 1970s helped to lay the foundation for this rediscovery.

The Charismatic Renewal as Trinitarian Correction in the West

The charismatic renewal arrived in Britain during a period of heightened secularization and individualism, and its brand of experiential, congregational worship took root quickly. Its influence was felt not only in the independent churches, but the historic denominations too, leading to a radical shake-up of evangelicalism.[17] It helped to revitalize the role of women and lay people in general,[18] while also deepening understanding and fellowship between Protestants and Catholics.[19] The inevitable conservative backlash was met head on, and the newfound prominence of the position of the Holy Spirit was retained.[20] Chief among the tools of the new charismatic movement was a renewed understanding of the Trinity. Many naysayers re-evaluated their position in the light of the scriptural assertion of the sovereignty of the Spirit: 'the Lord is the Spirit, and where the Spirit of the Lord is, there is freedom' (2 Corinthians 3.17);[21] and when faced with the undeniable freedom with which these Christians worshipped, it was clear that if fellowship were to be maintained, compromises would have to be made. Furthermore, this new spirituality modelled unity in diversity well, and seemed to be leading to a deeper understanding of the faith that would transcend the divisions of the Reformation. Leaders such as David Watson and Michael Harper began to moot the idea that the Reformation was in fact a tragedy that could have been avoided, rather than a much-needed corrective.[22]

Bretherton and Walker attribute the new insights of what they call the 'Deep Church movement', to the insights of C. S. Lewis. In a letter to *The Times* they wrote:

---

17 Bretherton and Walker, *Recovering*, pp. 5, 6, 7.
18 *Ibid.*, p. 6.
19 *Ibid.*, p. 7.
20 *Ibid.*
21 *Ibid.*
22 *Ibid.*

To a layman, it seems obvious that what unites Evangelical and the Anglo-Catholic against the 'Liberal' or 'modernist' is something very clear and momentous, namely, the fact that both are thorough-going supernaturalists, who believe in the Creation, the Fall, the Incarnation, the Resurrection, the Second Coming and the . . . Last things. This unites them not only with one another, but also with the Christian religion . . . Perhaps the trouble is that as supernaturalists . . . they lack a name. May I suggest 'Deep Church'.[23]

Bretherton and Walker attribute Lewis's *via media,* or middle way position, to the work of the Anglican divine Richard Hooker.[24] As I will explore later, Hooker helped the Anglican Church discover an ecclesiology that would unite both Catholics and Protestants in a single theological framework. The vision was one of unity in diversity, and as we will discover later, very much informed by Trinitarianism. Additionally, as Ramsey and Terwilliger point out, the renewal was about more than just unity, and a deepening of the experiential dimension of worship; it encouraged a deeper intellectual engagement too:

There is more to the Spirit than being moved, either as individuals or in groups . . . we need an intellectual experience of the Spirit as much as an intellectual experience of the Christ. In this enterprise we must return to the sources, to the New Testament, the Fathers and the Eastern Christian tradition, and from all this begin again. We need the Holy Spirit to enlighten us about the doctrine of the Holy Spirit – this will be truly a 'new theology'.[25]

Unfortunately the newfound ecumenism was to break down somewhat in the 1970s, succumbing to the factionalism of conservative Anglo-Catholics and evangelicals. However, real change had been

23 *Ibid.,* p. 2.
24 *Ibid.,* p. 3.
25 Ramsey *et al., Charismatic Christ,* p. 70.

achieved, and it was here to stay. Innovations such as the alternative worship movement and the Emerging Church grew out of the aspirations of the charismatic movement, with a passion to express worship and community in the context of the 'real world' of consumerism and pluralism. Alongside this, many other charismatic evangelicals continued to explore the concept of 'Deep Church'. More recently, the Anglican and Methodist Churches have seen the emergence of 'Fresh Expressions', an initiative that seeks to encourage contextual forms of mission and church. It is clear that a renewed understanding of the Trinity, and in particular of the role of the Holy Spirit, is leading to greater innovation and contemporary expressions of church. So where is all this leading?

The Age of the Holy Spirit and the Church

One way of understanding history is as the unfolding story of God's self-revelation. The Creator led the perichoretic dance of God from creation to the coming of the Redeemer.[26] During his ministry, the Redeemer led the dance with participation from the Sustainer and the Creator. Finally, the Sustainer leads from Christ's ascension until the Redeemer comes again. We live in a time of 'now, but not yet', an in-between time when the Kingdom of God has only been partly realized. This is a difficult period for the Church, and relying on the Holy Spirit doesn't guarantee we will get it right, as history has shown. Nevertheless, this time of divine open-endedness, which began at Pentecost, is what Zizioulas describes as the actual constitution of the Church. This is distinct from, and follows, the institution of the Church by Christ. The challenge for the Church is to take the nature of its existence seriously, and trust in the guidance and counsel of the Holy Spirit, following wherever God may lead. The vision for the Age of the Spirit, outlined

---

26 Where the Creator led, but the Redeemer and Spirit participated. Note: I am not saying here that there was no evolution other than God's hand was in whatever happened.

in 2 Corinthians 5, is for the restoration of all things into right relationship with God. Each Christian, as a temple of the Holy Spirit, has an ambassadorial role to the world; we are the medium through which the Divine mysteriously makes appeal to the cosmos for restored relationship. Teresa of Avila grasped this when she cautioned her fellow Sisters that when people praise them for their good works, or loving kindness, they were really praising the God that they encountered through them.[27]

Divine Open-endedness

You may find yourself asking, what about eternal life? Isn't heaven the ultimate point of fulfilment in the Christian life? The Cappadocians don't seem so convinced. They seem to have thought that the restoration of all creation into full relationship with the Trinity, or *theosis*, was the end goal of the journey.

Theosis
Is the understanding that the Christian spiritual path takes the disciple into an ever-deeper relationship with God. At its deepest, Christians become inseparable from God. The fulfilment is not that Christians become part of God, but rather grow spiritually to enter into inseparable relationship as an initiative of God's mission of love to the world, and through individual personal choice to take the Christian spiritual path.

Their scriptural foundation for such claims lay in the epistles, and such passages as 2 Peter 2. They argued that such a position was the logical conclusion to St Peter's claim that we will be partakers of the divine nature.[28] That's not to say that we actually become God,

---

27 As recorded in R. Williams, *Teresa of Avila* (London: Continuum Press, 2004), pp. 106–7.
28 Bretherton and Walker, *Recovering*, p. 16.

but that we will experience the fullness of relationship with the Divine for which we had been created, in all of its healed wholeness. This is put beautifully in 1 John 3.2:

> Beloved, we are God's children now; what we will be has not yet been revealed. What we do know is this: when he [Christ] is revealed, we will be like him, for we will see him as he is.

This is not to say that God becomes fully revealed, or that we are to lose the sense of mystery surrounding God's being; rather that we will experience the state of relationship that is the fulfilment of what it means to be human. For those in doubt, another reading of Paul's epistles is encouraged. While I do believe that one day we will live in a restored heaven and earth, I confess that many interpretations of the 'end times' and the afterlife make me deeply uncomfortable. I do not foresee it having overmuch to do with togas, harps, clouds or grapes; rather I suspect that it will be the fulfilment of what already exists: the restoration of the cosmos to its potential through relationship with the Triune God. Personally, it requires that I trust in the love of God, and continue to journey through life in the hope that I will be drawn deeper into who I am called to be. I am reminded of a story that Mike Riddell told at the Epicentre Network, an alternative worship community in southwest London. He was leading a day of exploration into what might help maintain the spiritual life in the cultural context of postmodernity. He talked about a profound experience he had had of God in a nightclub while out with some friends. The bar was crowded and the atmosphere was vibrant. Many people were dancing. Three people in particular caught his eye. They were quite drunk, cross-dressed men, and they had begun dancing very enthusiastically on top of the bar. On the face of it, this was arguably a most profane, irreverent scene. Nevertheless, Mike recalled having a very profound sense of God's presence in that very moment; it was unmistakable. He was deeply moved by the experience, feeling drawn into a sense of worship, awestruck by something of the beauty of God revealed in these men. Our Trinitarian God likes to mix it up: who's in the Kingdom, who's not; what's a sacred space, what's not, etc., etc. Trusting in this God who loves the marginalized, the sinners, the undeserved and the unlovely, through a profoundly open-ended faith, gives me hope in my own salvation and the salvation of all those I love. It comes down to relational trust in the generous love of the Triune God.

The Trinity and Kenosis

Kenosis connotes the sense of 'giving a gift' or of 'pouring out'. We encounter this 'pouring out' between the persons of the Trinity: the Creator pours out into the Redeemer and the Sustainer, and God pours out love into humanity and the whole of creation. Eastern Orthodox theology emphasizes that we are called to follow the example of Christ, and to pour out ourselves in loving others, growing in humility and in union with God, or *theosis*. This is the process of becoming alike to God, or in fact, developing holiness within us. Kenosis is a concept that provides a deep connection with the wisdom of the sixth and seventh centuries, helping us leapfrog the dry rationality of the Reformation and engage with the Spirit on a transformative experiential level. By pouring out ourselves in the way we see modelled in the Trinity, we share in God's nature and help to bring all things back into relationship with God. It is a great shame that the Church in the West has not understood or appreciated this aspect of God's nature.

Gospel as Open-ended and Unwritten

None of what I have said so far is beyond criticism. I have followed a particular argument, one that I believe to be true, but that has been greatly criticized by those of a more conservative and Western theological perspective. One of the most common arguments made against this position is that the gifts of the Spirit were given to the Early Church to constitute the Church, but then died out once it had become a stabilized institution. How, they argue, have we been able to exist as a church for over a millennium without them? This is arguably a strong position; however, it is weakened for me by the rational, logical and absolute conception of the nature of God that often accompanies it. The resultant beliefs in the inerrancy of the Bible, and the idea that we do not need any further revelation from God as we have all we need in the Bible (sometimes called the cessation of revelation in Christ) are very difficult to account for in contemporary society. This assumes we know everything, and that God cannot do anything new. Such a position recalls the idolatry of the fundamentalist conception of faith talked about in Chapter 1, where the ideas and symbolic representations for God become synonymous with God. This diminishes a full understanding of the Trinity because it fails to recognize the role played by the Spirit, and the equality of the person of the Perfecter within the Godhead. Trinitarianism preserves the ineffability and mystery of God, asserting that God cannot ever be fully known. It therefore also guards against the idolizing of scripture. The implication is also that God can change, and we see this in the differences between the Hebrew and Christian scriptures. The Bible is important within Trinitarian thought, but it is not the last word. As history marches on, God continues to work out the divine purpose, and we continue to learn more about that God. In this sense, the gospel can be understood to live within us, as our lives become part of the continually unfolding canon of scripture. We must have confidence in the Holy Spirit to guide and direct us into all wisdom, not to contradict scripture, but to bring new interpretations to light. The Spirit will provide ongoing wisdom and understanding with regard to the many areas the Bible does not make direct reference to, and to the few it does. So rather than living in fear, we should have confidence, in all we do, that God is before us, behind us, above us and below us, and that ultimately, our calling is to catch up with what God is already doing.

Reflection

In this chapter I have argued that the Western Church has been
distorted by an incomplete understanding of the person of the
Holy Spirit. I have also suggested that this has resulted in the division we see throughout its history. I have argued that the charismatic renewal, when combined with insights from the Eastern
Orthodox tradition, acted as an important corrective to this distortion. These insights have reframed my understanding of prayer,
worship and church and have helped me see what discipleship is
all about. They have also challenged the idolatry of the fundamentalist viewpoint, and provide for a more complex, transcendental
and mystical understanding of the nature of God, where God retains full autonomy.

4

Our Becoming through God

A favourite religious movie of mine is Kevin Smith's *Dogma* (1999). One of the early scenes introduces a character that is the epitome of the traditional church leader. He is concerned with plummeting church attendances, attributing them to the Church's failure to engage people with the real person of Christ. He goes on to say that the Church needs a more contemporary Jesus, a Jesus people can relate to. The resulting character, of which they produce a rather trendy statue, is dubbed 'Buddy Christ', who is shown smiling, winking and giving the thumbs up. It's a hilarious send-up of an all too familiar problem: the nature of the person of Christ has always been something the Church has found impossible to reach consensus on. In fact, it is second only to the Triune nature of God in the list of befuddling, vertigo-inducing theological chestnuts. Having spoken about the Sustainer in some detail already, we will therefore turn to an exploration of the person of the Redeemer, and after that, to the person of the Creator.

The Nicene Creed conceptualizes Christ as having a dual nature, so that he is both human and divine in equal measure. This is clearly paradoxical: how can one being be both divine and human? Most of the heresies of the Church have been the result of errors in emphasis of either one of these natures. Faithfulness to scripture requires that we appreciate this duality, and see Christ as a both–and paradox. Recent Western church history indicates that the balance has tipped in favour of Christ's divine nature. Productions such as *Jesus of Nazareth* (Zefferelli, 1977) and *The Passion of the Christ* (Gibson, 2004) demonstrate this well with their characterizations of Christ as an omniscient being, impassive to the rigours of physical hardship. The image presented here is akin to the children's picture-Bible portrait of Christ as meek and mild, resting reverently in his transcendent divinity, veiled thinly by his physical body. A truly human Christ could never be so neat and tidy, as we mere mortals can easily testify. Jesus surely experienced the full gamut of emotions and personal crises that the average person does in the passage of their days. I do find it fascinating that so many Christians struggle with the humanity of Christ, and seem to think that even raising questions about it is a sign of irreverence or unfaithfulness. Films such as *The Last Temptation of Christ*, which creatively explores the idea that he was tempted with sexual and relational fulfilment, pose a huge problem for many Christians, many of whom are sure to make their views heard in the media. Personally, I found the *The Last Temptation of Christ* a breath of fresh air, and when it did stray from the biblical narrative it was always to emphasize Christ the man. Denying or trivializing the humanity of Christ constitutes a lack of faithfulness to scripture, and only serves to alienate us from him. Over the course of his life, Christ grew into his true nature; he was, like us, a 'human becoming'.

However, he was no ordinary human being. Indeed, no ordinary human becoming would be so unpredictable, or so mysterious and *other*. In the sense understood within the apophatic tradition, Christ seems to have been impossible to really pin down, or make sense of. It was easier to talk about what he wasn't. Even though he took the bodily form of a human being, he seemed to play by different rules. This is so much the case that even now, two millennia since he walked the earth, we are still trying, and failing, to fully appreciate him. We see this in the way he talked in parables, a literary device that brought new metaphorical meaning to his listeners. Jesus as the Word reflects the character of God. When we speak, we reveal our personality and our character. In the same way Jesus is the expression of the immanent God, God with us; what some have called 'the ground of our being'. Jesus was fully human and fully God – both–and. But he is never fully knowable, despite what more fundamentalist Christians may believe. Ironically, they are not attending to the gospel stories, as it is impossible to hold this position if you actually read the scriptural texts for themselves.

From the dual nature of Christ arise the two great theologies of the Christian faith: incarnational theology, which emphasizes the humanity of Christ, and redemptive theology, which emphasizes the divine nature of Christ. In incarnational theology we encounter Christ the servant, the lover of people, who cared for the poor, the children and the marginalized. We encounter the Christ who performed miracles so as to include those excluded from society; essentially, the Jesus that we encounter in the gospel stories, who is physically present in the world. It has a high regard for human culture, the need for social justice and the desire to see the Kingdom of God realized in the here and now. It is strong on valuing our common humanity, on inclusivity and the practice of love. Conversely, it has a history of having a low regard towards repentance and obedience. Redemptive theology, which focuses on the divinity of Christ, has a high regard for Christ's call to repentance and to discipleship. It has a high regard towards scripture and obedience, conversion and faithfulness, while at the same time has tended to have a low regard towards culture, of downplaying our common humanity, human rights and social justice. The image encountered in the book of Revelation of Christ as King is the predominant conception of God.

These two theologies have divided the Church into Traditionalists and Progressives, Catholics and Protestants, for centuries, where too great an emphasis has been put on either the divinity or the humanity of Christ. The great sadness is that both these theologies are important and true. The Church for centuries has forgotten that we need a both–and approach, otherwise we distort not only our understanding of Christ, but also of the Trinity and ultimately of the Church. We will explore later how the Emerging Church seeks to correct this, emphasizing both–and, out of a desire to be true to the nature of Christ, and also reflect the Trinitarian foundations of the faith. The irony remains that if the Church is to be true to the full nature of Christ, Traditionalists and Progressives, Catholics and Protestants, must all stick together. We need to have a high regard towards being human, culture, social justice and inclusion, as well as towards scripture, redemption, discipleship and repentance.

We must remember the insights of the apophatic tradition, that God will never be fully knowable, and strive not to over-simplify Jesus. He will never be our 'best friend'; such a view will never be sustainable, and the truth is much deeper. In his book *The Complex Christ*, Kester Brewin rightly challenges simple solutions to the understanding of the nature of God and the role of church. He challenges the Church to explore afresh what it means to be a 'body of Christ' in the twenty-first century. We need to be very careful how we tell the story of God as Creator, Redeemer and Companion, and always maintain the truth that the Redeemer, while enfleshed as a human being, was never fully knowable, and so retain the mystery of his person.[1]

Paul Tillich coined the metaphorical phrase 'ground of our being' to describe God's incarnation as the Redeemer.[2] This key concept for our post-secular context draws on existential thought, and is a reaction to a faith that had become objectively certain and described in absolute terms. Existentialists believe that human beings define their perception and understanding of the world from experience, distrusting empiricism and approaches focusing on absolute truth. They believe that reality transcends scientific approaches. So Tillich advances the metaphor of Christ informing our identity as the 'ground of our being', thereby emphasizing the immanence of Christ. Therefore, as Tillich would have it, we ultimately perceive reality through the experience of God.

---

1 K. Brewin, *The Complex Christ* (London: SPCK, 2004), Chapters 1–3.

2 P. Tillich, *Systematic Theology Volume One* (London: University of Chicago Press, 1973), pp. 116–17, 155–8, 234–6; R. M. Pomeroy, *Paul Tillich: A Theology for the 21st Century* (Lincoln: iUniverse, 2002), pp. 1, 12–13, 22–30.

Stuart Murray is one of many writers to have commented on how the Nicene Creed jumps from the nature of Christ's birth to his death, saying very little about his life.[3] He argues that the profound teaching Jesus gave concerning how we should live has not been emphasized, particularly regarding the challenging of injustice and meeting the needs of the poor:

> The Nicene Creed, for instance, says Jesus 'was incarnate by the Holy Ghost of the Virgin Mary; and was made man. And was crucified also for us under Pontius Pilate.' It ignores his human life, moving straight from his birth to his death. Where are his miracles, relationships, teachings or subversive lifestyle? As in many fourth-century documents, where is Jesus? The other creeds contain this same startling omission.
>
> Explanations can be offered – creeds cannot include everything and the human life of Jesus was not something fourth-century theologians were debating, so this was not included. But this is precisely the point: Jesus' life and teaching were no longer the focus of attention. Christendom [the Church] was comfortable with a divine Jesus – and with belief that Jesus was also human – but struggled with the challenging reality of that human life. Though the creeds declare his humanity, this seems little more than an abstract philosophical principle . . . Jesus was worshipped, but not followed. This has left a lasting legacy . . . Jesus [as human] was consigned to the margins.[4]

The incarnate Redeemer challenged the rich young man, the might of Rome, the powers of the Jewish temple and its priests, with another way of being. We see this explicitly with his suggestion of civil disobedience concerning the Roman army. When asked about what to do when a soldier hits you, Jesus' recommendation to offer the other cheek is politically subversive, because it would

---

3 S. Murray, *Post-Christendom* (Carlisle: Paternoster Press, 2004), pp. 123–4.
4 *Ibid.*

force the Roman soldier to hit you with the inside of their right hand, and thereby acknowledge you as their equal. Further, when Christ directs his disciples to take the soldier's pack an extra mile, he is also being subversive, because it was illegal for a Roman soldier to ask this. There is much more in the Sermon on the Mount that is profoundly challenging and political. So when someone says that you should never mix Christianity and politics, you need to challenge them. It may not be in the Nicene Creed, but it is very much part of our calling to follow the way of the human Christ as believers. The Christian faith should relate to the details of life, not just to what we might think. In the words of the Redeemer, we find direction as to how we should live, consistent with a radical yet loving form of discipleship that has a high view of justice and inclusion, modelled on the perichoresis.

Implications of the Creator

One of the great tragedies of Western thought is its misunderstanding of the relationship of God with humanity and creation. Traditionally Genesis 1 is interpreted as God giving humanity the right to subdue creation rather than be stewards of it.[5] This has progressed to an understanding that creation is little more than a resource or a commodity to utilize. There has been a general lack of understanding of the important connection between creation and the Creator. Since the Enlightenment, the most common understanding in the West has been that God is a kind of watchmaker, who set the cosmos going and then stood back, only to reappear briefly in Christ.[6] The danger of this position is that it validates the view that the created order is little more than dirt,

---

5 P. Harrison, 'Subduing the Earth: Genesis 1, Early Modern Science, and the Exploitation of Nature', *The Journal of Religion*, vol. 79, no. 1 (London: University of Chicago Press), pp. 86–109.

6 J. Zuck, *Biblical Panentheism*, accessed 1.11.2011 at http://www.frimmin.com/faith/godinall.html.

and has no spiritual value. There is an acknowledgement that creation shows something of the handiwork of the Creator, but little more.

Pantheism

The belief that all nature and God are identical. Pantheists do not believe in a personal or Creator God. This is thus contrary to Christian thinking.

Panentheism

The belief that God exists and interpenetrates every part of nature, and timelessly extends beyond as well. All created matter is mystically connected to God, but God is not created matter.

The Eastern Church frowns on pantheism, believing that God, as the Holy Spirit, is transcendent and other to creation, but at the same time present to sustain it in its being. In this view God is not of creation, but is present to creation. The Eastern churches have a more *panentheistic* theology, where God is understood to be omnipotent, eternal and other, and yet present in all creation, enabling it to exist. Put another way, God's energy maintains all things and all beings, even if those things have explicitly rejected God. Because of God's love for creation, God does not remove the divine presence from it. (As an aside, this is not the same as pantheism, which says that creation is all that God is.) So rather than creation being just dirt, there is a mystical relationship between all matter and the Divine. Thus once more we meet the Holy Spirit, sustaining all life and matter in partnership with the Creator and Redeemer in the perichoretic dance of God. God is seen as the 'affect and effect' of the universe. It has been impossible for Western theology to go this far, as it has not had a developed understanding of perichoresis or of the role and person of the Holy Spirit. Only with these in place can panentheism be understood.[7] It could be argued that we in the West have plundered creation through a diminished understanding of the connection between creation and the Creator, and only now, in a time of acute environmental crisis, are we waking up to the importance of ecological stewardship and justice. Only now are we beginning to understand scriptural texts that talk of all creation groaning and waiting for redemption.[8] The cosmos has a touch of the sacred, reflecting the awesome beauty of the Creator who continues to sustain it, despite our best efforts to destroy it. This is not dodgy theology as argued by some conservative theologians; on the contrary, it is another aspect of the Christian faith that has remained underdeveloped in the Western Church. The environmental crisis we face has helped Western theology to catch up with some of the thinking prevalent in Orthodox theology. I hope never again to see Christian environmental campaigners labelled dodgy liberal do-gooders. It is quite reasonable to be moved by the beauty of creation, and as a keen surfer I find it easier to worship God in the midst of the beauty of the ocean and the coast than I do in many church buildings. I am constantly moved by a sense of God's Trinitarian presence in nature. This natural revelation is also an important stepping stone for people to encounter the living God. Although, to my distress, many Christians still fail to see the connection between faith and environmental stewardship, the Emerging Church, alternative worship, and Deep Church movements do seem to have gained and recontextualized some insights from the Eastern faith tradition. This is beginning to change our behaviour in that we are starting to seek ecological and environmental justice through stewardship. It is my hope that this will eventually affect global politics. We need it very soon!

7 R. Totten, *The Worldview of Panentheism*, accessed 10.11.2011 at http://www.worldview3.50webs.com/panentheism.html.
8 Romans 8.22.

By implication we are invited, in worship, to participate with the Creator, Redeemer and Companion and therefore also with all created matter. We join in with God, and the whole universe, in a truly cosmic understanding of Christian worship. Many alternative worship groups have experimented with this idea in eucharistic liturgies, drawing inspiration from the created, sacramental realm, to make God present through the bread and wine. Their mystical services, entitled, for example, 'Cosmic Eucharist' or 'Creation Eucharist', have been opening up this whole area as an authentic expression of Christian worship. This has been an important innovation in an age of increased interest in spirituality and mysticism.

This form of worship is not just about encounter with God; it is profoundly about how we live. One way of interpreting Genesis 1 is as God making a covenant with humankind, so that we become co-stewards of our planet and the universe. Covenants were ancient agreements between groups of people (e.g. two tribes) that were eternally binding, and included ceremonies where people became 'blood brothers' by cutting each other and sharing each other's blood as a sign of commitment. This is where we get the idea of the Old Covenant or Hebrew Covenant, and for Christians, the New Covenant in Christ. If Genesis 1 can be interpreted as a covenant, then our worship of God should include how we behave towards creation. In this way, recycling, using renewable energy, getting rid of your polluting car, are all authentic expressions of worship. Worship of God is about how we live as well as the more mystical and transcendent elements of encountering God.

Finally, I want to make some links between all that we have learnt so far. We see that the Holy Trinity is an interpenetration of the three persons of the One God, a dynamic, perichoretic relationship, the outworkings of which are love, perfect justice and inclusion. Therefore, the kenotic pouring out of God from the Creator to the Redeemer and the Spirit is shared not only with us, but also with the whole of creation. God can thus be understood to interpenetrate and sustain all creation in a panentheistic manner. There is a deep connection between all these concepts, whose common root is the Creator within the Trinity. It is in the Creator that perichoresis, kenosis and panentheism find their origin in the context of the Trinitarian God. There is deep symmetry here theologically, something we in Western thought and theology are still learning about.

Knowing through the Spirit

We have already extensively explored the implications of the person of the Holy Spirit in Chapter 3, but there are a few more things to say. We have called the Holy Spirit the perfecter of our faith, but how does this work in practice? How does the Holy Spirit perfect things? I want to argue here that imagination is very important, and that we need a theology of the imagination, where insight is gained from an emerging sense of spiritual experience. When you think about it, when we pray and when we worship, we do actively engage our imaginations. This is evidenced by the sense of awe and transcendence we occasionally experience. Imagination can be the meeting place between us and the Holy Spirit. You could argue that committed forms of spiritual reflection are about being open-minded and open to the promptings and insights of the Holy Spirit. This is why John Taylor in his famous book called the Holy Spirit the 'Go-Between God', who invites us to re-imagine and re-encounter God. Our imagination becomes the place for seeing new potential and new concepts, as well as the place where we meet and encounter God through the Holy Spirit. As we explored in Chapter 1, the parables used by Jesus illustrate this point well. They have deep metaphorical meaning and encourage us to understand through enabling us to re-imagine. This is understanding through experience, or knowing God through experience of God, as opposed to knowing God through facts. This form of knowing will always be emerging because new knowledge or language comes out of the interplay of the Holy Spirit with our imagination and experience. It is in this profound way that we are led into new understandings, new appreciations. Some of this approach does exist within the history of the Western Church, principally through the Quaker tradition. Quakers do not give sermons in the traditional style, but wait together for the Holy Spirit to speak through various individuals, in the form of thoughts, images, or impressions upon the imagination. This is not unlike what happened at some of the charismatic services I have experienced. It is easy to mock, but I do like the open-endedness of this approach, seeking the involvement of the Holy Spirit. It doesn't have to look so wacky either. Deep theological reflection can be open to this just as much as that which is more emotional.

Many recent books, including Kester Brewin's *The Complex Christ*, have focused on the idea of emergence and the emergent. Brewin's book focuses on the body of Christ as a metaphor for the Church, which he argues is distorted by hierarchical forms of leadership and by having paid workers, including priests. For Brewin, church should be a community of participation, with flat leadership structures. I cannot agree with all of this, but he is right to desire a church that is participative and that fully reflects the perichoresis of the Trinity. What I find particularly fascinating about his book is that he challenges the Church to look at the organization that occurs in nature. For example ant nests were thought to be top-down organizations, but really they are self-organizing, emergent communities, where different individuals are given different roles. He points out that cities, too, operate under processes of self-organization, and no one person is in control of movement or of where people work. He considers it possible for the Church to become a self-sustaining emergent organization as seen in nature. A panentheistic theology of nature indicates that there is something of God's hand in these natural organizations. Such organizations can be understood to find their dependency on the Holy Spirit so as to be able to form self-sustaining emergent communities. The great advantage of this could be the empowering of the people of God, the laity, to be the Church, moving away from passivity and 'church going' to participation and 'church being'. It is still possible to be this form of church, with division of labour and specialization, where people are given leadership roles but where all are equal, as a form of flat leadership. The main advantage of this for the Church is the shift from being an institution, back to being a community. The main disadvantage appears to be that you can only do this with a limited number of people. Nevertheless, if we are sincere about seeking ways of being church as community, there is a lot of wisdom in what Brewin is saying.

All the various church movements since the Reformation started out as a movement of the Spirit, and a desire to live out an expression of church that was more communitarian and partici-pative. Although I think the division caused by the Reformation is regrettable, I sense that many were driven by God to seek a more perichoretic understanding of God, with a participative Church, having flat leadership and far more of a vibrant community. It may be that it is the Holy Spirit that seeks to retain the sense of a participative community in the Church, and so limit the tendency towards institutionalization. This is something I think the Holy Spirit still beckons the Church to be today.

The Emerging Church and the Holy Spirit

There has been much written on the Emerging Church and I can-not hope to summarize it fully here. I will say that I consider it to be an authentic expression of church that seeks to be contextual, par-ticipating fully in the more postmodern and post-secular aspects of culture. What is of key interest here is whether it is a genuinely Holy Spirit-led reconstitution of church for a new expression of culture. Many of the people I have known who have been involved in the Emerging Church have come from some experience of the charismatic tradition. While many still have a strong understand-ing of the Holy Spirit's participation in the world and their lives, they are progressively more mystical in that understanding. The beginnings of the Emerging Church suggest that it may be such a

Holy Spirit-led innovation. Murray identifies 'emerging churches' beginning in the late 1990s as:

> An apparently spontaneous phenomenon ... without central planning, coordination, or consultation. Loose networking, shared stories, 'blogging' on websites and developing friend-ships were all that connected otherwise isolated initiatives ... The churches that have emerged in the past few years have been remarkably diverse. ...[9]

> Many emerging churches ... were not intended to become churches but developed into churches as those involved found their ecclesiology transformed by engagement with the community they were serving ... They grew into churches as those involved found the culture gap between new Christians and church too wide.[10]

For some emerging churches there is a temptation to be defined by what they are not. However, for a number there is a real Trinitarian basis to their identity, and as such they are spiritual communities that reflect the need for participation, creativity and inclusion. One of the first books written on the Emerging Church by Larson and Osbourne sets out a clear vision for a focus on 'unity in diversity', with a both–and mentality that seeks to reverse the fragmentation of the Church.[11] It is therefore a synthetic style of church, draw-ing on both incarnational and redemptive theologies. Larson and Osbourne note the following themes:

- Rediscovering contextual and experimental mission in the Western Church.
- Not restrained by institutional expectations.
- Open to change and God wanting to do a new thing.

---

9 S. Murray, *Church after Christendom* (Carlisle: Paternoster Press, 2004), pp. 69–70.

10 *Ibid.*, p. 74.

11 B. Larson and R. Osbourne, *The Emerging Church* (London: Word Books, 1970), pp. 9–11.

- Use of the key word 'and'. Where the heady polarities of our day seek to divide us into an either–or camp, the mark of the Emerging Church will be its emphasis on both–and. For generations we have divided ourselves into camps: Protestants or Catholics, high church or low, clergy or laity, social activists or personal piety, liberals or conservatives, sacred or secular, instructional or underground.
- It will bring together the most helpful of the old and the best of the new, blending the dynamic of a personal Gospel with the compassion of social concern.
- It will find its ministry being expressed by a whole people, wherein the distinction between clergy and laity will be that of function, not of status or hierarchical division.
- Due emphasis will be placed on both theological roots and contemporary experience, on celebration in worship and involvement in social concerns, on faith and feeling, reason and prayer, conversion and continuity, the personal and the conceptual.[12]

If this is truly the vision behind the Emerging Church and the Deep Church movements, and the driving force in the Fresh Expressions movement, then it may also be truly of the Spirit, who desires to perfect us and draw us back not just into restored relationship with the Divine, but to restored relationships with other Christians.

Reflection: Visual Expression of the Trinity

So far I have used many words to articulate an understanding of the Holy Trinity as Creator, Redeemer and Sustainer. Now it is time to explore this visually. Below is a Greek copy of Rublev's icon of the Trinity, which is centred on the mystical story of Abraham and the three angels. After reading the explanation below, I invite you to sit

---

12 *Ibid.*

with the icon as an act of worship with God. To see a colour copy of this icon on the Internet, go to http://www.ianmobsby.net.

The image reflects the story in Genesis of the encounter between Abraham and the three angels that mysteriously become God. The image begins with the three persons as angels, hence the wings. This is important, as according to Orthodox tradition, it is somewhat idolatrous to image the Creator who remains unrevealed.

In the centre is the Creator God. Behind this person is the tree, signifying creation, the tree of life, and also the tree of death. Sitting to the right of the Creator is the Redeemer, to whom the other members of the Trinity bow their head in respect. Behind the Redeemer is the tower of Babel, signifying humanity's rebellion against God. On the other side of the Creator is the Sustainer, who is coequal with the Creator and the Redeemer. Behind the Sustainer is Mount Sinai, the place where Abraham was tested with the potential sacrifice of his son Isaac. It is also the place of the temple and of Jerusalem. Before the great symbols of the Hebrew Covenant we meet the Holy Trinity, expressing one-ness. They model perfect love, justice and inclusion. As you look at their faces for a minute, imagine the kenotic pouring out of God into God-self. This icon is incomplete until you recognize that you are being beckoned to join with the three persons of God, relationally, and as an act of worship. Finally, in front of the perichoresis of God, we encounter the symbols of the New Covenant of God. In ancient tradition, the bread is already mixed into the wine, in the cup. So finally this icon draws you, through the sacraments, into worshipful relationship with the divine tri-unity. Just like everyone before, the icon draws you to worship God so that you join with the whole timeless communion of saints. Look at the feet. They are poised for movement, as if preparing to dance. This is not a God that sits still. Our challenge is to keep up with this God. So sit with this icon for a while.

Ian Mobsby and Tim Dendy

5

Models and Lessons from the Emerging Church

In 2005 I completed research exploring how emerging communities operating within an Anglican context were being authentically church. It became immediately obvious that Rublev's icon of the Holy Trinity was immensely important for all four of the Emerging Church projects I spent time with. It was used as a visual image incorporated into event flyers, or for alternative worship meditations, or just in the general worship life of the various communities. Further, it was found in offices, over work desks, in homes – everywhere, in fact. It was clear that it was bringing profound theological and social meaning to those involved in the various projects. Two of the projects opened all their services with an invocation to the Holy Trinity. Whether they were conscious of it or not, a developed Trinitarian understanding of God was evident in this worship. As I looked deeper, it became clear that all the groups I was researching appeared to have a profound understanding of the Trinity that was informing how they were church, where church is understood functionally as the activity of worship, mission and community.[1] All the groups had a strong sense that mission was about catching up with what God was already doing. Many of them were engaging with spiritual tourists, and in so doing, sought the presence of the Trinity in unlikely places. One

---

1 Ian Mobsby, *Emerging and Fresh Expressions of Church* (London: Moot Community Publishing, 2007).

of the most profound examples of this, which took place at many Mind, Body and Spirit festivals, concerned the exploration of the Trinity through the imagery of tarot cards. All the groups had a profoundly ancient:future focus that was refreshing and invigorating. They believed that the Triune God was present in all parts of life, and in all places. There was a strong sense of the person of the Holy Spirit being present as the Companion and Sustainer, something you do not hear much of in many Western churches. Further, some of the groups articulated a profound desire for a model of church that reflected the relations of the Trinity as a participative and creative community.

For my first book, *Emerging and Fresh Expressions of Church*[2] (the compilation of my MA research dissertation), I interviewed a number of participants committed to Emerging/Fresh Expressions of church to explore how their ideas of being church compared theologically and sociologically. A year later, Eddie Gibbs and Ryan Bolger produced the book *Emerging Churches,* drawing from a PhD thesis on the Emerging Church and a collection of personal stories, including my own. They interviewed a great number of participants of Emerging Church projects in Europe and the USA, all of which held the same seven core values. Many of those involved had never personally met, other than through websites and blogs, so it was astounding that there was so much consensus. The values of the Emerging Church were identified thus:

1 Who take the life of Jesus as a model to live (life as spiritual journey).
2 And who transform the secular realm.
3 As they live highly communal lives.
4 Welcome those who are outsiders.
5 Share Generously.
6 Participate.

---

2 *Ibid.,* pp. 50–68.

7 Create.

8 Lead without control (unity in diversity).

9 And function together in spiritual activities.[3]

I was given the opportunity to reflect on these findings when Ryan Bolger presented them to a gathering of Emerging Church leaders in the UK. I asked those gathered the question: 'Where do these values come from? How has so much consensus been reached?' I then suggested that perhaps the Emerging Church had found, or been led to, a Trinitarian ecclesiology that had inspired a particular model, the values of which reflected God's desire for what the Emerging Church should be. This is what Miroslav Volf talks about in his book *After Our Likeness*:[4] a church whose values reflect the Trinitarian God. This development appears not to have been a consciously chosen action, but to have emerged out of the experience and practice of those involved in the particular projects. Is this a Spirit-led re-imagining of church? Personally, I believe it is too much of a coincidence to say otherwise. If you look at these values for just a minute, they very much speak of a church modelled on perichoresis and kenosis.

Value One: following Christ as a model of discipleship. This connotes the sense of human becoming, discipleship, and church as a group of disciples seeking to live out together what Christ called us to.

Value Two: the transformative pouring out of God from the sacred into the ordinary. The Church reflects this call to worship God and in so doing pours out itself in loving action, mixing up the sacred and secular in the pursuit of transformation drawn from the love of God.

---

3 E. Gibbs and R. Bolger, *Creating Christian Communities in Postmodern Cultures* (London: SPCK, 2006), pp. 44–5.

4 M. Volf, *After Our Likeness: The Church as the Image of the Trinity* (Cambridge: Eerdmans, 1998), pp. 191–220.

Value Three: as God lives in perichoresis, belonging and love, so the Church is called to express community, belonging and mutual love.

Value Four: practising hospitality. As the Holy Trinity seeks to draw people into relationship with the Divine, so should the Church seek to love and draw into relationship those outside of itself.

Value Five: as the perichoretic Triune God interpenetrates the God-self in participation, love and inclusion, so the Church should be a generous, sharing community.

Value Six: as with God's perichoretic nature, where the three persons participate in God's oneness, so should the Church participate and include everyone as an expression of the Church's oneness.

Value Seven: as God creates and sustains the cosmos and inspires human development, so the Church should encourage creativity and development in all those involved.

Value Eight: as the Trinity models unity in diversity, where all three persons are co-equal, so should the Church reflect the sense of being a body of co-equal persons in one community.

Value Nine: as the Holy Trinity playfully and dynamically engages with the cosmos, so the Church should in its togetherness host spiritual activities.

In short these values appear, to me at any rate, to be informed by a Trinitarian ecclesiology – whether people are aware of it or not – and it is probable that the use of Rublev's icon brought about a shared theological meaning, modelling an expression of church to which they all aspired.

What is Driving these Values?

If I am right, and I believe that in this area I may be, the Holy Trinity is beckoning the Emerging Church to model a way of being a spiritual community that reflects the very nature of the Trinitarian Godhead. The Holy Spirit is drawing those seeking missional and contemporary expressions of church for our post-modern consumerist context, to experiment with forms of church drawing on a perichoretic model. As an aside, I remember that I first encountered the theological significance of Rublev's icon at a worship event led by Dr Luke Bretherton, where he led a meditation on it. Luke has been one of the key contributors to the Deep Church movement. Further, in a lecture by Prof. Andrew Walker of Kings College, London, to ordinands at St Paul's Theological Centre, the icon was used to illustrate the meaning of perichoresis. Andrew is also a key player in the Deep Church movement. Therefore, I now think that this icon may also have opened up a whole depth of meaning, not only to the Emerging Church network but also to the Deep Church movement. I love the idea that this icon may be the Holy Spirit beckoning us on, transforming our imaginations, and helping us re-imagine another way of being. Taylor puts this eloquently:

> Any attempt to image God contextually is in fact an act of God reading us. As we embody God, as we proclaim God in community, God looks back, questioning the church: Is the church fully representing the image of God? Is the church a participatory place where people find their full humanity in Christ? Is the body of God a true icon of God? . . . Will we let the image of God construct us?[5]

It is clear that this form of thinking, of the Church reflecting the nature of God, has deeply influenced a number of writers involved in postmodern theology or ecclesiology. As Tillard writes:

---

5 S. Taylor, *The Out-of-bounds Church? Learning to Create Communities of Faith in a Culture of Change* (Grand Rapids: Zondervan, 2005), p. 71.

Ultimately then, we enjoy the fullness of community as, and only as God graciously brings us to participate together in the fountainhead of community, namely, the life of the triune God . . . The community that is ours is nothing less than shared participation – a participation together – in the perichoretic community of Trinitarian persons.[6]

In the end, participation in the perichoretic dance of the triune God as those who by the Spirit are in Christ, is what constitutes community in the highest sense and hence marks the true church.[7]

But is this scriptural, I hear you cry, this concept of the Church modelled on the nature of the Trinity? Volf argues that this form of church as participation in the communion of the Triune God (which brings hope and present experience) has a strong New Testament basis. Further, he implies that this concept of church appeared to 'emerge':

New Testament authors portray the church, which emerged after Christ's resurrection and the sending of the Spirit, as the anticipation of the eschatological gathering of the entire people of God . . . The eschatological fulfilment of the high-priestly prayer of Jesus, (John 17:21) I ask . . . that they may all be one. As you, Father are in me and I am in you, may they also be in us.[8]

Furthermore, the mutual giving and receiving in such a mystical community is modelled on the Trinity, which is mutually abiding and interpenetrative:

---

6 J. M. Tillard, *Dilemmas of Modern Religious Life* (Delaware: Michael Glazier, 1984) in S. J. Grenz, 'Ecclesiology' in K. J. Vanhoozer (ed.), *The Cambridge Companion to Postmodern Theology* (Cambridge: CUP, 2003), p. 268.

7 Grenz, 'Ecclesiology', p. 268.

8 M. Volf, *After Our Likeness*, pp. 128–9.

So that you know and understand that the Father is in me and
I am in the Father.

John 10.38, 14.10–11, 17.21[9]

Volf also argues that the Church prefigures, albeit dimly, the eventual eschatological restoration of all creation into relationship with
God (1 Corinthians 12.4–6).[10] So there is a strong New Testament
basis to this form of church. To explore this further we must turn
to the work of Avery Dulles.

Models of Church

In his key book, Dulles explores a number of different models of
church, from across the various denominations, each reflecting
various aspects of the nature of God, and of Christ in particular.
It is my view that the models corresponding most accurately to
the normal functioning of the Emerging Church are the 'Mystical
Communion Model' and the 'Sacramental Model'.[11] This is borne
out by the qualities of Rublev's icon, which we have seen is so important to the Emerging Church community. It not only models
the kenosis and perichoresis of God, but is also set in the context
of the sacrament of Holy Communion. I'll explore both of these
models in greater detail.

Mystical Communion Model

This model of church is centred on a sense of community that
reflects the Godhead in perichoresis. Church then is more of
an interpersonal community rather than an institution. It is a

---

9 *Ibid.*, p. 208.
10 *Ibid.*, p. 235.
11 A. Dulles, *Models of the Church* (New York: Doubleday, 2002), pp. 39–54,
55–67.

fellowship of participating individuals, brought together through God and in particular through Christ. The I–Thou relationship with God is a gift of grace, rather than a demanding one of obedience and good works. The model connects strongly with the mystical 'body of Christ', a communion centred on the spiritual life of faith, hope and charity. The model resonates strongly with Aquinas's notion of the Church as the principle of unity that dwells in Christ and in us, binding us together and in God. It consists of equal persons drawn together to journey spiritually with one another in God. Mission becomes the activities that dispose people to an interior experience of belonging and eventual union with God effected by grace.[12]

Dulles sees this form of church as empowering its members to fully participate in the life of the spiritual community, as they are animated by supernatural faith and charity, and led into communion with the Divine.[13] Because of its fluidity, Dulles believes that this form of church is good at adapting and responding to social change. Regarding traditions of church, this model is open to both Protestant and Catholic:

> In stressing the continual mercy of God and the continual need of the Church for repentance, the model picks up themes of Protestant theology . . . [and] in Roman Catholicism . . . when it speaks of the church as both holy and sinful, as needing repentance and reform . . .

> The biblical notion of Koinonia . . . that God has fashioned for himself a people by freely communicating his Spirit and his gifts . . . this is congenial to most Protestant and Orthodox . . . [and] has an excellent foundation in the Catholic tradition.[14]

---

12 Dulles, *Models*, pp. 44–53.
13 *Ibid.*, p. 50.
14 *Ibid.*, pp. 46, 50–1.

It is therefore unsurprising that this framework enables the Church to reflect the both–and vision of the Emerging Church, drawing on the best of the Catholic and evangelical traditions in a new, or should we rather say old, synthesis. It is an expression of faith that reflects the relational and mystical quality of spirituality that arises out of the postmodern elements of our culture. I will look at this more closely in the next chapter.

There are, however, a number of disadvantages to this way of being church. Firstly, because of its organic nature, it can be difficult to define where church begins and ends. There is a danger of over-spiritualizing and deifying the activity of this type of church. If the Holy Spirit were conceived of as the life principle of the Church, then all actions of the Church would seem to be attributed to the Holy Spirit. This obscures the personal responsibility and freedom of the members. In such situations there could arise issues relating to the abuse of power, resulting in unhealthy forms of community.[15] The greatest weakness of this model is that it can undervalue the significance of Christ as a human being, where everything becomes too mystical. The incarnational aspect of Christian faith is therefore most at risk with this model. There is also the danger of seeing your own form of church as the only or most legitimate, with the resultant loss of the sense of the wider catholic church. Finally, this form of church tends to neglect the organizational aspects of the Church. The accountability and transparency of church authority and governance is therefore at risk of compromise. As in the sociology of cults, charismatic people can assume leadership and power where governance structures have not been established. Thankfully most emerging churches have addressed the need for structure and models of leadership, but it remains a weakness of the model, and as such remains a work in progress. However, I have also met these very same problems in more traditional forms of church.

---

15 *Ibid.*, pp. 44–53.

Sacramental Model of Church

The notion of church as sacrament is Dulles's second model of church. In this typology, the church becomes an event of grace as the lives of its members are transformed in hope, joy, self-forgetful love, peace, patience, and other Christ-like virtues.[16] A sacrament is a sign of God's grace, of God's gift. It is socially constituted, a communal symbol of grace coming to fulfilment. The main advantage of this second model is that sacrament becomes a visible sign of the presence of the revealed God, so that spectators may encounter God, or at least recognize the significance of the Church as a numinous sign. For most church traditions, the climax of sacrament is expressed in Holy Communion or Eucharist, with people gathered around to eat the bread and drink the wine. The Church becomes a local expression of the gathering of all people, brought together through the presence of God, as Christ commanded at the Last Supper: God's mystical transcendent presence made immanent. The implications for mission are profound, when God is understood as being made present by the activity and presence of Christians in local communities. It is clear that some emerging churches have made this connection:

> A gift of the emerging church is that we see God equally in the Eucharist and in drinking beer together in the local bar.[17]

> Emerging churches tend to have rediscovered a more sacramental approach to everyday life . . . we gather around weekly Eucharist . . . We try to take a sacramental view of the whole of creation . . . A sacramental life is a life lived in God, so each day is sacramental and we ourselves are sacraments of God in the world . . . A defining characteristic of church has to be the regular participation in the community in Eucharist.[18]

16 *Ibid.*, pp. 55–63.
17 Mobsby, *Emerging and Fresh*, p. 60.
18 *Ibid.*, p. 59.

You may notice that this last quote makes connections between the sacramental and panentheism. This is no coincidence; there is a real connection between the idea of God's blessing through his presence in the bread and wine, and in the sustaining power of the Spirit in nature. When the sacraments are understood in combination with perichoresis, kenosis and panentheism, the relationship between God, the Church and world becomes an expression of God's presence in and commitment to the world. This understanding is somewhat neglected in the Western Church. The Church is instituted and constituted by the Trinity, and commissioned to acts of worship, mission and community in loving service to God in the world. By drawing on these two models of church we have an authentic expression of church, the deep theological meaning of which resonates with the vision and values of the Church.

Ekklesia and Transformative Community

The concept of the body of Christ as used by the Apostle Paul connects with his use of *ekklesia*, a New Testament word meaning church, or literally a 'gathering or assembly of people'.[19] It is also understood to reflect the idea of an alternative community, one that seeks to embody the values of the 'now but not yet' Kingdom of God.[20] It is a community that does not seek to remove itself from the world, but rather to transform it, as Christ did through his ministry and the ministry of the disciples.[21]

[The Church] as the new social organism, springing from the words of Jesus in calling the twelve, with a citizen body which

---

19 P. Ward, *Liquid Church* (Carlisle: Paternoster Press, 2002), pp. 6–9; B. A. Harvey, *Another City* (Harrisburg: Trinity Press International, 1999), p. 150.

20 Grenz, 'Ecclesiology', pp. 257–60.

21 Harvey, *Another*, pp. 15–16, 25.

scandalously included from the beginning slaves, women and even children, persons, who had no place in the traditional ecclesia ... obeyed his [Jesus'] new commandment to love irrespective of blood ties or social class.[22]

The original *ekklesia*, from which the Early Church derived its meaning, was an alternative to the town council or local legislator in the Greek-speaking parts of the Roman Empire,[23] and was ruled by the wealthy male elite. The Church sought to be an alternative *ekklesia*, and therefore it included the powerless, such as slaves, the poor and women, within its ranks.[24] It sought to live out the Kingdom in the 'now but not yet', on social, economic and political levels, including the spiritual.[25] As a consequence, those once excluded from society were 're-membered', or included in the Church.[26]

Christianity entered history as a new social order ... From the very beginning Christianity was not primarily a 'doctrine', but ... a 'community' ... a New Community, distinct and peculiar ... to which members were called and recruited ... Primitive Christians felt themselves to be closely knit together ... in a unity which radically transcended all human boundaries – of race, of culture, of social rank, and indeed the whole dimension of 'this world'.[27]

22 R. C. W. Chartres, 'Ecclesiology' – Edmonton Area Conference 15-vi-2004, accessed 11.11.2011 at http://www.klisia.net/blog/BishopoflondonaddressEcclesi ology-EdmontonAreaConference.15-vi-2004.pdf.

23 P. Avis, *The Anglican Understanding of Church* (London: SPCK, 2000), p. 1; Harvey, *Another*, p. 23.

24 Chartres, 'Ecclesiology', 2–3; M. Maggay, *Transforming Society* (Oxford: Lynx, 1994), pp. 31–3, 36–7, 49–50.

25 Harvey, *Another*, pp.17–22; Ward, *Liquid*, pp. 9–10.

26 Chartres, 'Ecclesiology', p. 3; Harvey, *Another*, p. 57; Maggay, *Transforming*, p. 15.

27 G. Florovsky, in Harvey, *Another*, pp. 21–2.

This concept of 're-membering' also makes connection with the sacramental understanding of the significance of the *ekklesia*: that at the Last Supper, Jesus re-membered the new *ekklesia* through the inauguration of the Eucharist or Holy Communion. To re-member symbolizes our coming together, and in so doing, our living out what Christ called us to be. Christ becomes alive to the world through us. Christ becomes present as we retell and live the narrative of God.

> The re-membering that Jesus commanded us to undertake was more profound than simply remembering past events. We are called to nothing less than a re-membering of Christ's body on earth having understood that everything in heaven and on earth should find their head and centre in the Word made flesh. In this way we are called into participation . . . in the round dance of the Trinity, the perichoresis.[28]

This original understanding of *ekklesia* has been somewhat lost because of the process of institutionalization that has since occurred. However, it is my contention that, whether consciously or not, the Emerging Church has rediscovered something of this understanding through the use of Rublev's icon. It is a model of church that draws on the strength of the mystical communion and sacramental models of church, with a focus on being an alternative inclusive community drawing on an understanding of *ekklesia*. The Emerging Church has come a long way!

The Wisdom of Richard Hooker

The Reformation in the UK is marked out as one of the more painful periods in church history. The expectation of unity in

---

28 Chartres, 'Ecclesiology', p. 3.

conformity throughout the Tudor period swung violently between Catholic and Protestant interpretations of what the true Church was. In this conformity model, Christians were literally killing each other. Some theologians appreciated the need for a more diverse Church, and sought an ecclesiology that somehow held both traditions in tension. Richard Hooker, an Anglican divine, was one of these.[29] His writings drew on both the mystical communion model and the sacramental model of church, to try to hold Catholic and Protestant together. He also drew on the perichoretic nature of God, adopting the Trinitarian model of community as unity in diversity, with a broad centre.[30] In *The Laws of Ecclesiastical Polity*, Hooker's Trinitarian ecclesiology attempts to hold both Protestant and Catholic in tension, and yet also exclude fundamentalist expressions at either extreme. Why is this important? Firstly, it is saying that an understanding of the Trinity has helped the Church to deal with difference and unity. This both–and approach is therefore not new. Some Emerging and Fresh Expressions of church are rediscovering resources that have a tradition within some of our historic denominations.

Fraternity as New Monasticism

A mixture of emerging churches, Fresh Expressions of church and mission initiatives arising out of the charismatic traditions have begun describing themselves as new monastic communities. They again draw on a combination of the mystical communion and sacramental models, with a core concern to engage with the question of how we should live. The most successful of these have experimented with a combination of church centred on place and network, with intentional communities, cafés and centres to practise hospitality. Many also have a rhythm, or rule

---

29 I go into a lot of detail on this in my first book, *Emerging*, pp. 69–72.
30 *Ibid.*

of life to express what it means to be a Christian in a post-secular context.

A rhythm or rule of life

Originally conceived by monastics and friars, rhythms or rules of life were aimed at assisting young Christians to develop and sustain a rhythm of spiritual wellbeing in daily life. New Monastic communities have opened these up for spiritual seekers to engage with the question 'How do we live in contemporary culture but not of it?'

The early Christian monastic and mendicant orders, such as the Benedictines and the Franciscans, modelled how to be both–and communities, by drawing on a mystical communion model of church. Both in their time were fresh forms of church, which sought simultaneously to be radical new communities practising companionship and hospitality, and as participating, accountable members of the wider Mother Church. Both religious orders expressed a fraternal approach to church as a reaction to the increasingly institutional church they were accountable to at the time. They practised the radical counter-values of powerlessness and poverty. In this way they attempted to be radical alternative communities to the church they were part of, while relating missionally to the contemporary culture of their times. This was a culture of mysticism, superstition and the spiritual, and their Christian spirituality was an attempt to recontextualize the faith in an intelligible way. In a similar way, new monastic communities are attempting to relate to a culture of spiritual mysticism in a twenty-first-century context, modelling expressions of the Christian faith that can relate to this culture. I will explore this culture of mysticism more explicitly in the next chapter.

For the purpose of this book, I want to draw on what has been learnt from the emerging forms of new monasticism: specifically, Church of the Apostles in Seattle, USA, mayBE in Oxford,

Safespace in Telford and the project in London with which I am personally involved, Moot.

Flat Leadership and Collaborative Decision-making

One important structural value of both old and new monastic communities is the sense of fraternity or belonging to a college. Traditionally, would-be members join the local chapter and make a full, annual commitment to a rule or rhythm of life; new monastic communities have also taken up this practice. The chapter is given support and guidance by elected priors, and the abbot or abbess, who also look after administrative matters. Some have different levels of belonging, so that a spiritual path from the third to first order of belonging can be followed. In both old and new forms there is a strong sense of shared decision-making and leadership, so that roles and responsibilities are exercised by all within one co-equal community. Such roles are performed as a matter of function, not of power or privilege. This interpretation of a mystical communion model corrects a weakness regarding visible governance structures, and therefore some emerging churches have adopted it. Some, like Moot, have opted instead to adopt a rhythm of life as an aspirational statement, to which all are encouraged to commit at an annual service before the Bishop of London on Holy Saturday, during Easter Week. This clearly reflects a perichoretic understanding of church.

Rhythm of Life

Many of the emerging new monastic communities have reinterpreted the ancient form of a rule or rhythm of life. They seek to answer the question 'How should we live?' rather than 'What should we believe?' This is a particularly important approach because it expresses what the Christian faith means in practice, encapsulating the values of discipleship, social, economic and ecological justice, balance and spirituality, all in the context of the fusion of the mystical communion and sacramental models. To demonstrate this, I will list the Moot Community's rhythm of life, created in 2007.[31]

> We live the moot rhythm of life through presence, acceptance, creativity, balance, accountability and hospitality.

> presence
> We commit to journeying together with God and each other, by meeting together as a community, in prayer, in worship, friendship, grief, and happiness. Being a hopeful sign of an open community in the city rather than just a group of individuals or anonymous people.

> acceptance
> We desire to accept both ourselves and other people as they are, and to allow people to say what they believe without fear of judgment. We want to create a safe space where people feel at home and welcomed. We hope to learn from all those in and outside the community.

> creativity
> We want to have an open approach to how we learn, live and encounter God in the plurality of our city and the world. We wish to be creative in our worship, in prayer, in our lives, in learning, and with the Christian tradition, in our theology and with the arts.

> balance
> We aspire to live with integrity in the city, striving as a community for balance between work, rest and play. We wish to develop healthy spiritual disciplines such as daily prayer,

---

31 http://www.moot.uk.net – accessed 1.11.2011.

meditation and contemplation, drawing on the ancient Christian paths. We want to live within our means, living sustainable lives. We desire to not be simply consumers, but people committed to giving and receiving in all of life.

accountability

Within the rhythm of life we desire to be accountable to one another, to grow and journey together, listening to each other and the wider Christian community for wisdom rather than trusting only ourselves. We want to have a willingness to share life, rather than to privatize it and we seek to walk together in a deep way rather than as strangers who only know the surface of each other.

hospitality

We wish to welcome all whom we encounter, when we are gathered and when we are dispersed, extending Christ's gracious invitation to relationship, meaning and life in all its fullness.

This rhythm of life is an innovative way of expressing the Christian faith in the context of contemporary culture. Some visitors have expressed their concern that such rhythms of life are not explicit concerning the nature of God or the more traditional Christian confessional message, but this is surely missing the point. As people encounter Christians living out profound expressions of faith through God's love, they encounter the depth of a loving Christian community and experience God as their ground of being, through worship, mission and community. Such an approach explicitly trusts the Holy Spirit to bring meaning and spiritual experience to people as they encounter Christians living out their faith in the ordinariness of life. It is in these participative and loving Christian communities that people can encounter the reality of the Christian story of the Holy Trinity, not as hypothetical truth, but as a profound reality, clueing us in as to how we should live.

Participation in Doing

The key value of these forms of church is that they are totally dependent on the involvement and shared leadership of the people of God in acts of loving service. People are not merely involved; they actually lead various activities, and thereby help to fully express the dynamic of a spiritual community. This conception of church as a participative spiritual event reflects the Trinitarian understanding of God as an event. This keeps the Church healthy, as such forms of church are only as good as the relationships that comprise them; moreover, people learn more about God through spiritual experience and encounter than by the acquisition of facts.

Mission Consideration

This approach to being church is fully open to the postmodern pursuit of learning through experience. Simply learning facts about God is an inadequate approach in contemporary culture. Traditional forms of church usually hold to the pattern that says that belief is a necessary prerequisite for belonging. In a postmodern context this effectively excludes many people. If people need spiritual experiences to work out if, and what, they believe, then an approach that enables people to belong to such communities as unbelievers is crucial, if we are to be committed to appropriate forms of mission and evangelism. This 'belonging without believing' is a core value of emerging church communities, and it is made increasingly possible through the use of rhythms or rules of life. Such an approach trusts in the inspiration of the Holy Spirit revealing the nature of God to those who are not yet Christian. In this way God, through new forms of church, draws people into restored relationship with the Divine, helping them shift from spiritual tourism to Christian pilgrimage.

89

Reflection: Why are these Models of Church Important?

In our postmodern context there is a desperate need for models of
church that are able to function within and relate to contemporary culture, and which express the truths of Christianity through
loving service. Whether we like it or not, some current forms of
church, and the faith they express, are anachronistic and do not
help people encounter the deep love of God in a positive, health-
giving form.

What I cannot understand is how some forms of church express so much hatred, hardness and elitism, making the love of
God seem such a long way off. Much preaching appears to appeal
to the power of guilt and shame rather than loving inspiration. I
am sure that this is due in part to fundamentalist expressions of
faith, where everything must be kept black and white. We must
resist simplistic solutions in our expression of church, and em-
brace the necessary complexity of living out our faith in a complex
world. A dear friend, who was told a lie in the name of the supposedly loving Christian God, helped bring this home to me most viv-
idly. After years of trying to make a failing marriage work, through
counselling, marriage guidance and prayer ministry, he reached
the point where there was nowhere else to go. Having decided,
after much heartache, to get a divorce, he sought out the pastor at
his local church for guidance. He was told that what he was about
to do was wrong, and that the Church did not have a duty to support Christians seeking divorce. He was further informed that he
was removing himself from the love of God, and from the Church
by his actions. He was effectively excluded from church and from
God (as he understood it), because he was seeking pragmatic solutions to the very real problems of his life. My friend came to me
in the middle of the night and in deep pain and tears to ask, 'Will
God ever love me again?'

I can't express how angry this made me, both back then and
now as I recollect it. I told him, through my own tears, that God
had never stopped loving him, and that there was no such thing as

the doctrine of limited grace. This false teaching justifies the thinking of fundamentalist Christians and has effectively wrecked the spiritual and social lives of many people. The research I conducted for my previous book has convinced me that this approach to the Christian faith has successfully de-churched a great many people. The shame it creates often causes people to walk away from God, and to limit the power of the infinite love of God. No human being has the right to define who is in and who is out, when the love of God is concerned. Such beliefs must be challenged by those prepared to model alternative expressions of Christian community.

I believe that the large number of controlling leaders in the Church is a reflection of particular models of church. Too much unaccountable power in the hands of an individual in a hierarchical context often results in the institutionalization not only of the church community, but also its leader. Power always distorts; it's part of the darker side of our human nature. Christendom (which assumes a powerful and privileged position for church leaders), is a model of church with centralized and hierarchical power structures, created in a time of royalty and nobility. Such a model appears to me to be utterly anachronistic, a wholly inaccurate reflection of the idea of *ekklesia* – an alternative inclusive and participative community. We remember that Christian monasticism, an alternative Christian community and movement, was birthed in its resistance to the founding of Christendom. When Christianity became the official religion of the Roman Empire, monks and nuns escaped from such dominance into the freedom of the deserts of Alexandria and Syria to express an alternative Christian spirituality and community.

The models of church we have looked at seek to draw on the perichoretic nature of the Holy Trinity, as an alternative to some of the more aggressive forms of church. I do believe that God has led the Emerging Church in this way, so as to counter the increasingly hard-line, loveless forms of fundamentalist churches found today. Often these churches model a 'church as business' approach, which over time becomes hierarchical and oppressive, with leaders gaining enormous power. In so doing, they become the new Pharisees and Sadducees. There is a need to return to the values and forms of church modelled in the New Testament. It will be exciting to review what has happened in another ten years.

The Church needs to relate to the culture in which it finds itself, and we increasingly live in a world driven by information technology, consumerism and post-secular sensibilities. How does a church drawing on the relational and transcendent aspects of the Holy Trinity operate in such a world? I will explore this in the next chapter.

6

Ancient:Future Church

It was a warm spring day, and I was in the Royal Horticultural Hall in central London, at the annual Mind Body and Spirit Festival. The hall was divided up into over 150 exhibition units. The festival took the form of a trade show, offering everything you could think of in the name of spirituality and inner peace. Among the massage healers, crystals, auragram machinery and feng shui booksellers was the Dekhomai stall. *Dekhomai*, the ancient Greek word for 'the welcoming place', was the name given to a co-operative of a number of London-based Christians, which included members of Moot, some CMS employees, an alternative worship community, some Baptists, a few local Anglo-Catholic Christians, and a charismatic house church. Some Christians think that these festivals are for a fringe minority, but while this was the case in the 1960s and 1970s, it no longer holds in the twenty-first century. There is currently a renewed interest in all things spiritual, as opposed to traditional forms of religion. Two thousand people visited the festival each of the four days it was open, each paying over £20 just to get in: spirituality is no longer a minority sport. Inside, one could bang a gong for fifteen minutes and discover inner centredness; browse a variety of crystals, on sale at anything from £20 to £2,000, that would help channel your energy so you could sleep at night; or have your tarot cards read for £30. In the midst of this spiritual market place, a bunch of Christians put together a stall offering free massage, anointing with oil, prayer, and spiritual direction in various forms of Christian meditation – 'Christian spirituality to go', and free. I massaged feet, gave the occasional blessing, and just took the time to listen to and talk with whoever came along. It was an incredible opportunity to love people by listening to their stories, and to offer hope and prayer. Many were confused that our ministry cost nothing. Others couldn't work out how Christians, associated with the Church, could be so loving: surely there was a catch? Most came with a keen sense of their own pain, and visited each stall in a desperate search for authenticity and spiritual relief. As I massaged feet, people would relax and begin to open up, sharing their deep struggles, passions, desire to belong, desire for love, desire to be more human and less busy. In the midst of all of this I prayed and blessed people in the name of the Creator, Redeemer and Companion. People laughed, people cried, people were still, and people appeared to experience profound things of God in that little place. My hope is that our diverse bunch of Christians enabled people to encounter the Holy Trinity, and that God was able to pour out the divine love through us. It was precisely the place church should be, and in a form that made God accessible and authentic to the brave new world of spiritual questing in our culture.

Many in the Western Church have yet to realize that rather than succumbing to increased secularization and disbelief, spirituality has become an issue of exponentially greater significance in recent years. Unfortunately for the Church, this interest in things spiritual often excludes traditional forms of religion.[1]

The Rise of Holistic Spirituality and Techgnosis with the Demise of Religion

The Times published this bold headline in 2006: 'Christianity will be eclipsed by spirituality in 30 years, startling new research predicts.

---

1 There has been a lot of discussion about whether this is true, following a research project that explored whether young people going to a nightclub made any associations with religious imagery or ideas. The research showed that young people have no residual appreciation for religious ideas. Those critical of the research indicate that the research asked the wrong questions, which should have been orientated towards 'spirituality' rather than 'religion', and for which the sample size was quite small. For more information see http://easyasfallingoffablog.blogspot.com/2006/09/spirituality-of-generation-y.html–accessed 1.11.2011.

Our correspondent reports on the collapse of traditional religion and the rise of mysticism.'[2]

Mysticism

The pursuit of spiritual encounter or conscious aware-ness of an ultimate reality, or God, through direct experi-ence, intuition, instinct or insight. Mysticism usually focuses on practices intended to nurture those experiences or awareness.

It is questionable whether thirty years is an accurate prediction for the demise of Christianity, but the rise of mysticism as a form of spirituality is not. I'll clarify what I mean when I talk about spiri-tuality in this way. Yvonne Richmond has, in my view, given the best definition:

> 'Spirituality' has become an 'in' word; today it covers every-thing from different moral and ethical codes in a diverse range of esoteric, sometimes occult practices. It is largely influenced by Eastern religions and the New Age Movement, with their emphasis on attaining higher consciousness in the search for the divine, the interrelatedness of all things, and holistic heal-ing . . . people are looking for new solutions to the struggles they face.[3]

So rather than turning to atheism and secularization, our culture appears to be turning to a belief in mysticism. This is supported

---

2 C. Midgley, 'Spirited away: why the end is nigh for religion', *The Times*, 4 November 2006. P. Heelas, L. Woodhead, B. Seel and K. Tusting, *The Spiritual Revolution: Why Religion is Giving Way to Spirituality* (London: Blackwell, 2007).

3 Y. Richmond, N. Spencer and S. Croft, *Evangelism in a Spiritual Age: Communicating Faith in a Changing Culture* (London: Church House Publishing, 2007), p. 8.

by research (Hay and Hunt, 2002) that looked at the changes in spiritual experiences or perceptions. The results are significant.[4]

Spiritual Experience/Perception	1987	2000	% Increase
A patterning of events/ transcendent providence	29%	50%	90%
Awareness of the presence of God	27%	38%	41%
Awareness of prayer being answered	25%	37%	48%
Awareness of a sacred presence in nature	16%	29%	81%
Awareness of the presence of the dead	18%	25%	39%
Awareness of an evil presence	12%	25%	108%
CUMULATIVE TOTAL	48%	76%	

These statistics show that something is changing in the UK's extremely cynical post-secular culture. The changes are, however, emphatically not in the favour of traditional religion, as the results of other recent research bears out very clearly.[5] The vast majority of people in the UK have either given up on church or never had anything to do with it.[6] This leaves a residual 20 per cent of people who regularly attend, where 'regularly attending' means one visit per month. Official statistics estimate that 40 per cent of the population of the UK is de-churched – meaning that they

4 D. Hay and K. Hunt, 'Frequency of report of religious or spiritual experience in Britain for years 1987 and 2000', qouted by D. Hay, 'Experience', in A. Holder (ed.), *A Blackwell Companion to Christian Spirituality* (Oxford: Blackwell, 2007), pp. 417–41; Richmond et al., *Evangelism*, p. 11.

5 Sources: BSA, 2004; European Social Survey, 2002; BgbF, 1996/7; Tearfund, 2005/6; ORB, 2005; Populas, 2006; HMSO, 2000; Christian Research, 2006.

6 P. Richer, *Gone But Not Forgotten* (London: DLT, 1998); G. Cray et al., *Mission-Shaped Church* (London: Church House Publishing, 2004), pp. 37–8.

have either drifted away from church due to changes in work or home circumstances, because of a bad experience of church leadership, or because they could not make any sense of the gap between their lives in the real world, and the world of church. This leaves a further 40 per cent who are non-churched: they have never attended a church.[7] Remarkably, however, many people still consider themselves to be Christian, but would express this more in terms of spirituality:

> In 2000, sixty percent of the population claimed to belong to a specific religion with fifty five percent being Christian. However, half of all adults aged eighteen and over who belonged to a religion have never attended a religious service.[8]

We see here the rise of a 'pick'n'mix', individualistic interpretation of religion, which is more about spiritual tourism, spiritual fulfilment, and the quest for inner peace and wholeness than participation in the Church.[9]

> The point of tourist life is to be on the move, not to arrive . . . there is no goal beckoning at the end of life's travels . . . impulse and spontaneity become the new control.[10]

This is not an easy journey for spiritual questers, or the traditionally religious among us. The sense of nihilism, disorientation, pain, insecurity and liminality is often acute. What we are facing

---

7 Cray et al., *Mission-Shaped Church*, p. 39; A. Jamieson, *A Churchless Faith* (London: SPCK, 2002), pp. 9, 16.

8 HMSO, *Belonging to Religion: Social Trends 32* (London: HMSO, 2000).

9 M. McCarthy, 'Spirituality in a Postmodern Era', in J. Woodward and S. Pattison (eds), *A Blackwell Reader in Pastoral and Practical Theology* (Oxford: Blackwell Publishers, 2000), pp. 193–6.

10 Z. Bauman, *Postmodernity and its Discontents* (Cambridge: Polity Press, 1997), pp. 90–4.

is the change of a paradigm, a change in the very way we perceive reality. As Lyon states:

> Traditional religious outlooks, with their fixed points, transcendent anchors, and universal scope, seem out of kilter with the emerging spirit of the age.[11]

To the pre-modern mind (before the Enlightenment) reality consisted in the God or gods above, and the devil or beasts below. There was a strong sense of the sacred and of transcendence, which we see reflected in the imagery of creation in Genesis 1. Spiritual experience and mysticism were an accepted part of everyday life. Modernist thinkers (from the Enlightenment until the mid-twentieth century) deliberately rejected transcendence and mysticism, seeing them as little more than 'hocus pocus' and superstition. Knowledge was divided between objective and subjective truth, where the subjective had no value. Emphasis was on objective fact; there was nothing more than the physical world, the observable here and now. During this time the mysticism of the pre-modern mind-set didn't disappear, it just went underground (however, both mind-sets continued to operate within the Church). This shifted again in the latter part of the twentieth century with the advent of postmodernity (also referred to as liquid modernity, more often by those who see the period of time in question as a continuation of modernity, rather than the beginning of a new epoch). People began to realize that those who proclaimed the objective as truth were not being fully honest, as all experience and truth is ultimately subjective. Therefore the central tenets of the scientific method are perceived to be increasingly less absolute. No longer objectively certain, knowledge is increasingly provisional, contextual and subjective.[12] The new postmodern

---

11 D. Lyon, *Jesus in Disneyland* (Oxford: Polity Press, 2002), p. 14.

12 M. P. Gallagher, *Clashing Symbols: An Introduction to Faith and Culture* (London: DLT, 1998), pp. 100–4. For more detail, see my book *Emerging and Fresh Expressions of Church*.

sensibility dictates the primacy of the subjective over the supposedly objective. Now in the twenty-first century, postmodernity has given way to post-secularization.

We live in a culture defined by consumption, pluralism, uncertainty, immediacy and individuality. This has become so pervasive that many people define themselves by the labels they wear, the cars they drive and the bars they drink in, creating a new pick'n'mix lifestyle.[13] So for those who have money, consumption has become the new strategy for defining one's identity. Immediately we can see how this excludes the poor; many young people have therefore turned to geographic, turf tribalism as a response. The great sadness of our times is the loss of a sense of common humanity, brought about by the culture of consumption. What happens when your partner dies, you lose your job, or you get depressed? What does one do with such a life strategy? Many of us indulge in a little retail therapy. We reinvent or re-affirm ourselves through a seemingly limitless supply of credit. Life is lived in the eternal present: 'live for today as tomorrow may never come'. It is a consumerist life based on the model of the eternal tourist who never arrives at their destination. So we travel light, trying to ensure that cumbersome commitments are kept to a minimum. As a solution, this doesn't go very deep, and when trouble hits, which it inevitably will, our patterns of consumption become addictive. The following two examples will illustrate my point.

The first concerns the two key characters in the film *Fight Club*, who meet at a number of twelve-step support groups for various addictions and health conditions. They start to tour a variety of different support groups with a view to encountering the real, raw emotion of suffering people, and the compassion, belonging and care shared between those in pain. They start regularly attending some of these support groups even though they do not

---

13 S. Taylor, *The Out-of-bounds Church? Learning to Create Communities of Faith in a Culture of Change* (Grand Rapids: Zondervan, 2005), pp. 24–7, 88; Z. Bauman, *Liquid Modernity* (Oxford: Polity Press, 2000), pp. 1–14, 53–63, 92.

suffer from any of the conditions or addictions the groups were set up for. The relief from stress that they experience helps them sleep at night.

The second example I would like to give is the opening story in an edition of *Adbusters* magazine. The inside front cover has a picture of a crying girl surrounded by bottles of alcohol and other consumer products. Above the picture is the title 'The quest for an authentic life', and the following lines:

> One glorious day, a girl sat down to write. Her mind was blank with only hazy thoughts. Her life was a joke, full of bullshit and filth. She was dirty in a dirty place. Who cares about her anyways? The room was empty, devoid of furniture or sign of life, besides the empty pizza boxes scattered around the room. Her life was trash, just like the room. Pain was her only true companion. Tears filled her eyes as she stared down at the blank paper. The coloured lines began to blur from the salty water. She sat still, wallowing in the depths of her infinite sorrow . . . Is this voice in the back of my mind fooling me? Am I really a unique human being with my own body, mind and soul, on my own magic journey of life? Or is this feeling of separateness an illusion, the source of all my anxiety and angst? Sometimes I'm afraid . . . I'll make a habit of presenting to be other people. There's the charm of the twenty-first century living, isn't it? Let's play make-believe! I'll make up life stories for entirely fictional characters, with fictional friends and fictional accents and fictional personalities.[14]

Both of these examples illustrate the point that, despite the illusion presented, consumption does not bring lasting spiritual relief. Instead it increases one's stress and the sense of liminality. And most importantly, it doesn't help answer the existential

---

14 A. Gill, 'The quest for an authentic life', *Adbusters Journal of the Mental Environment*, vol. 15, no 4, July/August 2007.

questions *Who am I?*, *Where do I belong?*, *What am I?* These unanswered questions drive people into a quest for meaning and belonging, often as spiritual tourists at events like the Mind, Body and Spirit Festival. The equally powerful and influential force of information technology also helps to drive this consumerist spiritual questing.

For those who can remember, think about what your life was like before fax machines, before laptops, e-mail, mobile phones, the Internet, and text messaging. Technology has transformed our lives into a constant flow of information; often all we can do is try to keep our heads above water.[15] We now live in a global village of immediate communication. The world of information technology has also opened us to the concept of cyber- or virtual reality. This means that the modernist concept of reality, all about the objective, the here and now of a purely physical world, no longer applies. There is a new sense of otherness and transcendence in the popular psyche, and it is mediated by information technology. Surprisingly, our highly technical postmodern culture has given life, once again, to something of a pre-modern mind-set.

Rollins, Caputo and Davis all attribute the renewed interest in spirituality directly to the reality of a new form of transcendence, a new spiritual belief in the impossible:

> The impossible has recently become possible again, that the very force of modernist criticism when turned on itself opens the way for a post-critical and post-secular posture that accommodates the passion for the impossible. That movement of living on the limit of the possible, in hopeful expectation of the impossible, a reality beyond the real, which I take to be the mark of a religious sensibility ... We live ... in a world of high-tech advanced telecommunication systems, a dizzying world that is

---

15 Lyon, *Disneyland*, pp. 13–14, 37; J. Caputo, *On Religion* (New York: Routledge, 2001) pp. 67–8, 76–7.

changing everything . . . Religion shows every sign of flourishing in a new high-tech form.[16]

Cell phones whose signals easily penetrate thick walls, satellites that link across the globe . . . we have found a way to mime the angels.[17]

We are faced with an amazing – shall we say an impossible? – situation: the simultaneous flourishing of science and religion,[18] and indeed, at its extremes, of advanced hardball science along with some far out screwball superstition. We live in a world where the most sophisticated scientific and high tech achievements co-habit . . . Fundamentalists, New-Age spiritualities, and belief in all sorts of bizarre hocus-pocus phenomena . . . However, there is increasing rejection of traditional forms of spirituality.[19]

Hyper-real spirituality

The seeking of a form of spirituality over and above the certainty of living in a highly scientific and technological culture. It is a form of questing for spiritual experience that transcends the physical world.

So this hyper-real[20] form of spirituality, the seeking of the impossible over the real, makes connections with pre-modern forms of mysticism, reframing them for a new postmodern and post-secular context:

---

16 Caputo, *On*, pp. 67–8.

17 *Ibid.*, p. 70.

18 I would argue that here Caputo means spirituality rather than religion.

19 Caputo, *On*, p. 70.

20 P. Rollins, 'His Colour is Our Blood: A Phenomenology of the Prodigal Father', PhD thesis (Belfast: Queen's University, 2004), pp. 117–20; E. Davis, *TechGnosis, Myth, Magic and Mysticism in the Age of Information* (London: Serpent's Tail, 2004), pp. 4–10.

So here we are: a hyper-technological and cynically postmodern culture seemingly drawn like a passel of moths toward the glittering flames of the pre-modern mind.[21]

Today's techgnotics find themselves, consciously or not, surrounded by a complex set of ideas, and images: transcendence through technology.[22]

Techgnotics

Those who have discovered a form of spirituality driven by the experience of modern information technology, often unconsciously.

In seeking answers to life's key questions, we find ourselves in a culture gripped by the search for transcendence and new (or rather I should say old) forms of mysticism. This is not a new situation; much of the pre-modern world was on the same quest. In fact, before the invention of the printing press, the Catholic Church constructed a form of liturgy that utilized all the senses, so as to engage with a world that was centred on mysticism. It is therefore unsurprising that alternative worship groups have often reframed ancient liturgies and resources like the Labyrinth, for use with a post-secular audience. The approach used is therefore often described as ancient:future.

The model of spiritual community used by monks and friars in the pre-modern era, characterized by radical inclusion and hospitality for spiritual tourists, has been a key source of inspiration for the new monastic movements of postmodern times. It is no coincidence that the British reality TV shows *The Monastery* and *The Convent* were hugely popular (these programmes charted the experience of a small group of people spending an extended period

---

21 Davis, *TechGnosis*, p. 5.
22 *Ibid.*, p. 122.

of time with a monastic community). This new, hyper-real spirituality undoubtedly presents something of an opportunity for the Church, but most likely not in its traditional form. The Church has a calling to help those who find themselves in the context of new mysticism, to shift from the endless path of the eternal spiritual tourist, to the purposeful journey of a Christian pilgrim.

Unsettling of the Spirit?

As Peter Rollins reminds us, the postmodern turn to the subject has helped us see that our very lives allow us to experience the Christian God as radically subjective. God's immanence is hyper-present, so that we encounter the Divine through the subjective experience of the presence of God in the ordinariness of our lives.[23] I would argue that this yearning for transcendence is the continuing work of the Sustainer and Perfecter, the Spirit of God. I would pose the question: might virtual reality conceivably provide for the possibility of an 'I–Thou' encounter? Have the vehicles of information technology and consumption, imperfect and flawed pursuits of humanity though they are, become an opportunity for a transformative encounter with the Holy Spirit? I believe this to be the case.

The Moot Community website now receives 15,000 hits per month, and most of these are from spiritual tourists.[24] There are often two or three new people at Sunday services who claim to have discovered us through the Internet. This is the case for many alternative worship and emerging church communities. And when you consider the number of services happening every month, that's a lot of people. Therefore I would like to argue, unlike some

---

23 P. Rollins, *How (Not) to Speak of God* (London: SPCK, 2006) pp. 23–4; Rollins, 'His Colour', p. 4–10.

24 These numbers are measured by online tracking software. This software also enables analysis of what subjects people were searching for. This data suggests the search for forms of spirituality relevant for spiritual searchers.

writers (such as Michael Frost[25]) that God is still present in the incompleteness and brokenness of the post-industrial, consumerist Western culture. What is absolutely not needed is a withdrawal from the world for fear of it being godless. The great danger of seeing oneself as separate from the world, as a stranger in a foreign country, is that it predisposes us to the 'sin of Holiness' that Riddell has warned us of. We develop a dualistic mind-set that says 'we are right and they are wrong'; this creates an attitude of superiority and certainty, which can lead to fundamentalism. The Church must never lose its trust in a God who is present in all of creation and in all cultures. When it does, it experiences distortion in its ministry. As Harvey stated:

> Christian communities must learn to deal with the problems and possibilities posed by life in the 'outside' world. But of more importance, any attempt on the part of the church to withdraw from the world would be in effect a denial of its mission.[26]

Such a withdrawal would undermine the both–and balancing act of holding incarnational and redemptive theologies in tension. Such a retreat into the overemphasis of redemptive theology would be to repeat the historical mistakes of the Western Church. The challenge for the Church is how to be in but not of contemporary culture.

I may be an overly optimistic, romantically minded Christian, but I believe it is possible to maintain such a radical theological tension; I also believe that our world, which seems increasingly violent and dehumanizing, needs it now more than ever. My own incompleteness compels me to hold onto the hope that the Trinitarian God is as involved in the world of the twenty-first century as much as any other time. I believe that the universe is

25 M. Frost, *Exiles: Living Missionally in a Post-Christian Culture* (Peabody: Hendrickson Publishers, 2006), pp. 81–104.

26 B. A. Harvey, *Another City* (Harrisburg: Trinity Press International, 1999) p. 14.

still inherently good and beautiful, and that humanity is still being beckoned into relationship with the Divine. Rather than spelling the end of religion, the concept of techgnosis gives me even greater faith in God's presence, and it encourages a belief in the impossible over and above what might seem rationally possible. After all, it was foundational for my own conversion to Christianity from a long line of atheists. There are, however, some downfalls to the new context of techgnosis.

The Danger of the Pick'n'mix God

At my lowest times, I fear that my ministry provides nothing more than a good exit strategy for falling out of relationship with the Christian God. I worry that I give permission for people to pick'n'mix a God of their choosing, watering the traditional doctrines down so that they fit obligingly with the individual's own pre-established values. In our current cultural climate, these are both very real threats. There is always the very real danger of binding God into a specific culture with post-secular consumerist sensibilities. Syncretism is a problem all Christians who seek to live in but not of contemporary culture must face. My greatest challenge is relating with those who define God by a set of consciously thought through consumerist processes, which tend to be self-centred, rather than mediated or led by God. It is much easier, for example, to believe in a pluralist god, so that all religions are equally valid routes to the same God. The inconsistencies and differences of approach in the different religions are smoothed over, creating a personalized 'my-spirituality': a dumbed-down, more palatable spirituality for the discerning postmodern, post-Christian consumer. That this approach undermines the Trinity and much of the narrative of the New Testament is a 'compromise that modern people should be able to bear'. Now don't hear me wrong: I do believe that there are truths in all religions and faiths, but I also believe that Christianity has the most distinctive (while imperfect) understanding of the Holy Trinity. It is this distinctly Christian narrative that renders the concepts of salvation, perichoresis and the rest possible. While I do think that God can use other religions to convey the Trinity, in my view Christianity retains the best imperfect understanding among other imperfect understandings.

Many spiritual searchers do wrestle healthily with God on an existential level. However, the danger is one of not really seeking God for understanding. As a culture we are terrible at listening to one another because our skill-sets are centred on consumption. Instead of attending to the other, the human ego retains the power to define God without any attempt to seek. Only by attending to the mystical otherness of God in humility, powerlessness, and contemplative and creative prayer, can I develop an adequate subjective comprehension of who this God is. It has always seemed paradoxical to me that often those who are wrestling with God do not believe in prayer, or any subjective spiritual experience other than 'conceptual thinking'. Their experience of God is almost entirely logical and of the mind, and mediated by the rigorous practice of certainty in their uncertainty. A high level of cynicism protects this position from any of the more positive outlooks on offer.

For some, this is a phase of deconstruction, a healthy part of the process of finding a deep faith of their own. God often leads us into desert experiences, so that we can reconstruct a more mature and God-led faith. The pattern of faith and doubt is a healthy expression of Christian discipleship. In fact, the Christian life can be a helix of ever-continuing circles of orientation, disorientation and reorientation. Put another way, it can be seen as a cycle of life, death and resurrection, eventually being led by God into a more mature faith. But healthy deconstruction does require deeper engagement through to reconstruction. However, some get stuck in deconstruction, and remain arm wrestling with God indefinitely. Only by finding what Paul Ricoeur calls a second naivety and Dave Tomlinson calls a second innocence, an ability to get beyond our doubts and thoughts, emotions and feelings, can you hear God for what God says. Only by letting go, and by acknowledging your need for God, will you allow God in. Douglas Coupland's book *Life After God* is the epitome of this.

One of the short stories in the book, '1000 years (Life After God)', has the main protagonist, Scout, reach the climax of his spiritual quest in the symbolic setting of a forest. He is so unhappy with his experience of the contemporary postmodern world that he has failed to return to work and is at his wit's end. He is clearly expecting something extremely significant to occur, and is open to the possibility of some sort of spiritual encounter. He spends the night in his tent, which is pitched in a very remote spot, near a pool by a waterfall, and he now awaits the dawn:

Here I now lie, on my stomach, looking out at the dark wet world, pulling the blanket tighter around me, smoking a cigarette, and knowing that this is the end of some aspect of my life, but also the beginning – the beginning of some unknown secret that will reveal itself to me soon. All I need to do is pray ... I kneel down and sip water from the pool. I raise my head and look through the clearing of the trees. I see the sun shining in the sky – a spinning ball of fire ... This same sun – the same burning orb of flame that shone over my youth – over ... swimming pools and Lego and Kraft dinners and malls and suburbia and TV and books about Andy Warhol ... I remove my blanket and fold it on the warm rocks beside the water. I then remove my shoes and socks and stick my feet into the water, and oh, it is cold ... And the water from the stream above me roars. Oh does it roar! Like a voice that knows only one message, one truth – never-ending, like the clapping of hands and the cheers of the citizens upon the coronation of the king, the crowds of the inauguration, cheering for hope and for that one voice that will speak to them. Now here is my secret: I tell it to you with an openness of heart that I doubt I shall ever achieve again, so I pray that you are in a quiet room as you hear these words. My secret is that I need God – that I am sick and can no longer make it alone. I need God to help me give, because I no longer seem capable of giving; to help me be kind, as I no longer seem capable of kindness; to help me love, as I seem beyond being able to love. I walk deeper and deeper into the rushing water . . . the water enters my belly button and it freezes my chest, my arms, my neck. It reaches my mouth, my nose, my ears and the roar is so loud – this roar, this clapping hands. These hands – the hands that heal; the hands that hold, the hands we desire because they are better than desire. I submerge myself in the pool completely. I grab my knees and I forget gravity and I float within the pool and yet, even here, I hear the roar of water, the roar of clapping hands. These hands, the hands that care, the hands that mould; the hands that touch the lips, the lips that speak the words – the words that tell us we are whole.[27]

This kind of surrender is key in moving from a simplistic, unsustainable faith, to something more complex, open-ended and sustainable. We need to constantly die to ourselves in order to be constantly born again in our walk with God. This is the walk of authentic Christian discipleship. If our life strategy remains purely consumerist, then we will not experience the incredible depths of God. It is by its nature a risky and uncertain journey, requiring us to let go of control. However, it can in equal measure be utterly resourcing and transformative.

Fundamentalism as the Impossible Faith of Techgnosis

This form of impossible, mystical spirituality is not all good news. The process of globalization itself can create forms of postmodern fundamentalism. Belief in the impossible can also create, in Caputo's words, an 'impossible people'. Fundamentalist forms of

27 D. Coupland, *Life After God* (London: Touchstone Books, 1994), pp. 355–60.

faith, oppressive, controlling and violent, can easily take root in our current spiritual environment.[28] Violence and oppression is so often the dark side of human passion. A strategy for dealing with the complexity of the world that is simplistic and black and white will always require some degree of violence and dehumanization to maintain it. The challenge for progressive Christians is to live out a faith that is characterized by the values of love, powerlessness, non-violence, inclusion, generosity and hospitality, in the belief that God works through these, albeit at great personal cost to us.

Reflection

Personally I do believe that God, through the person of the Holy Spirit, is beckoning us through the joint effects of consumerism and techgnosis. There is a real danger that both spiritual tourists and Christian pilgrims can become caught up with their own thinking and overly rational forms of certainty, which become more important than discerning experience. But having said that, our times offer a real opportunity to those forms of church that reflect a mystical communion and sacramental model, and take an ancient:future approach.

---

28 Caputo, *On*, pp. 92–3, 108.

7

Orthopraxis and Sacramentality

At a recent convention of emerging churches there was a discussion about sacraments and church:

> The emerging church is not shy about raiding the storehouses of the Roman Catholics, the Orthodox and the Anglicans for richer liturgies as well as prayer beads, icons, spiritual direction, lectio divina and a deeper sacramentality. The return to this ancient faith and practice is increasingly seen as a way forward in churches polarized by worship wars and theological intransigence. Thus, emerging churches often characterize themselves as 'ancient-future', a phrase that comes from a series of books authored by Webber (*Ancient-Future Faith*, *Ancient-Future Evangelism*, and *Ancient-Future Time*). This return to the past should not be confused with nostalgia for 1950s Protestantism or with a circling of the wagons around a purer Reformation theology. The return is deeper, looking to the treasures of the medieval and patristic theologies and to practices that have long been ignored by evangelicals.[1]

This ancient:future approach is part of an attempt to understand what it means to be Christian, drawing on the ancient to inform the current. This is not as easy as it sounds, and touches on what is called contextual theology, a much-maligned discipline by those of

---

1 S. Bader-Saye, 'A New Kind of Church', *The Christian Century*, 30 November 2004, pp. 20–7.

a conservative orientation. The task is difficult because you can't just take writings from the Cappadocian Mothers and Fathers about the Trinity, or scriptural texts, plonk them into post-secular cultures, and expect them to be understood and appreciated in their fullness. World-views, language, values and perceptions are totally different from those common in ancient times. So how and what the Church does with these ancient writings and practices requires careful consideration. Contextual theology takes culture and cultural change seriously and attempts to understand the Christian faith in context,[2] where the language of biblical theology often does not resonate with contemporary experience. It has been defined as:

> A way of doing theology in which one takes into account: the spirit and message of the gospel; the tradition of the Christian people; the culture in which one is theologizing; and social change in that culture.[3]

Barbour and Bevans propose that the various models of contextual theology attempt to create a symbolic system or framework to enable theologizing in context.[4] Models are understood to be logical theological positions that allow for some insights and connections. Each model differs in the balance it achieves between incarnational and redemptive theologies. Bevans proposes that there is a continuum between purely redemptive and purely incarnational focused models, and most models strike something of a balance between these two theologies.[5]

Part of the argument in my first book was that Emerging and Fresh Expressions of church appear to be utilizing a synthetic model of contextual theology, for a distinctly postmodern

---

2 S. B. Bevans, *Models of Contextual Theology* (Maryknoll, NY: Orbis Books, 2002), pp. 1–2, 5, 7.

3 *Ibid.*, p. 1.

4 Barbour as recorded in Bevans, *Models*, pp. 24–5.

5 Bevans, *Models*, pp. 24–5.

context.[6] This model attempts to listen to culture for basic patterns and structures, and thereby pinpoint the basic symbol systems in operation. Out of such a 'thick description' (holding many things in tension – scripture, culture and tradition) will emerge basic themes for the local theology. At the same time, however, these themes need to be in dialogue with the basic themes in the Gospels and tradition. This strategy, which holds on to the sense of an ancient:future faith, has a mutually transforming effect.[7] This particular relationship between church and culture relates to Niebuhr's synthetic approach, where 'Christ is above culture' but enters into it, and where culture is seen positively, as a vehicle for leading people to Christ.[8] Thinking about this again, I am left with a couple of questions. Where is the place for the 'I–Thou' relationship to bring transformative and subjective meaning out of the perichoretic nature of the Trinity? Where is the place for the meeting of the human imagination and the guidance of the Holy Spirit? These are not explicit in the synthetic model of contextual theology, but are very much present in another of Bevans's models, the transcendent model of contextual theology. I am therefore challenged to consider whether Trinitarian theology and an ecclesiology that is centred on perichoresis, kenosis and panentheism requires the use of a more transcendent contextual theological perspective.

Bevans considers the transcendent model to be more focused on incarnational theology (social change and culture), but influenced by redemptive theology (gospel message and tradition) as a starting point.[9] The model assumes that the development of a truly contextualized theology takes place as an individual wrestles with his or her own faith and shares that faith with others within the same

---

6 I. Mobsby, *Emerging and Fresh Expressions of Church* (London: Moot Community Publishing, 2007), pp. 28–30.

7 Bevans, *Models*, p. 86.

8 H. R. Niebuhr, *Christ and Culture* (New York: Harper & Row, 1951), cited in M. Percy, *The Salt of the Earth: Religious Resilience in a Secular Age* (London: Continuum, 2002), pp. 36–40.

9 Bevans, *Models*, pp. 26–9.

culture. It assumes a process of questing and questioning for 'what is'.[10] It starts with one's own religious or spiritual experience and life story. Exploration and encounter with God helps to articulate 'who I am' and 'who God is', as a product of subjective experience tied into a particular historical, geographical, social and cultural context. God's revelation is transcendent but revealed in human experience. For this to work, such models assume that humankind operates in identical ways in all cultures and in all periods of history, and that the self-transcending subject possesses effective and cognitive operations. Revelation then relates to a change of mind or thinking, literally a conversion from experience leading to a radical shift in perspective. This resonates with the phrase I have used repeatedly in this book: of 're-imagining another way' – a form of transformation. Such a contextual theology 'will not appear primarily in books, but in people's minds'.[11] In this model all Christian believers can be context theologians. The process of interpretation evaluates cultural experience against the Christian's experience of God.

Bevans outlines several advantages to this model. Firstly, it is a new way of doing theology – theology as activity. The historical and the cultural are genuine sources of revelation. The universal structure of human knowing and consciousness provides a common ground for mutual conversation and interaction.

The model has, however, not been without criticism. As Bevans indicates, some have criticized the process as too abstract and difficult to grasp. The assumption of the universality of human knowing has been questioned. It may be that such a view is a Western male assumption. The greatest danger of a subjective focus is that experience-led revelation may degenerate into relativity and utilitarian individualism, the very process that we are trying to find an alternative to. Having mentioned this, the general approach of this book is to emphasize that all of God's self-revelation is realized in the context of subjective human experience; this is a

10 *Ibid.*, pp. 97–104.
11 *Ibid.*, pp. 100–4.

core understanding of the Cappadocian Mothers and Fathers, and now of postmodern theology too. Through researching this book, I can now see that different Emerging Church communities are utilizing different models of contextual theology. Those of a more Trinitarian-influenced ecclesiology seem to be utilizing a transcendent model, while those more attentive to culture and emerging faith are utilizing a synthetic model. Both, however, stand quite opposed to what Bevans calls the 'translation model' of contextual theology favoured by those of a more conservative and overly rational sensibility. This form of theological engagement conforms to Niebuhr's 'Christ against culture', where culture is seen negatively as a distraction from Christ.[12] As a model of contextual theology, the translation approach emphasizes retaining Christian identity, as dictated by tradition, as more important than cultural identity. There is little awareness or acceptance that with this model, the Church needs to be immersed in a particular culture.[13] This approach could be accused of window-dressing or sexing-up the faith, where externally it may appear updated, but remains essentially unchanged. Rather than being a subjective 'I–Thou' encounter, revelation is more about communication of certain unchanging absolute truths or doctrines of God, and because they are from God they are wholly culturally free.[14] As Bevans says, there is a real danger of over-emphasizing knowledge of God through facts rather than God's self-revelatory presence:

We might criticize as well the translation model's implicit notion of revelation as propositional. Revelation is not just a message from God, a list of truths that Christians must believe. Revelation is the manifestation of God's presence in human life and human society, and the Bible represents the written record of that manifestation in particular times and within a particular

---

12 Niebuhr, *Christ and Culture*, pp. 30–9.
13 Bevans, *Models*, pp. 30–46.
14 *Ibid.*, p. 34.

society . . . the texts of the Bible are the results not of heavenly dictation, but of the struggles of women and men of faith to make sense out of that faith in the midst of lives where God's presence was often less than self-evident. Rather than a list of doctrines to be believed, the Bible – and to some extent the Christian tradition – presents various valid ways of wrestling with faith and doing theology.[15]

It is this absolutizing use of the creeds (such as the Nicene Creed), and defining who is in and who is out, that makes many contemporary Christians weary of dogma and the early creeds. But rather than give up the gift of the Cappadocian Mothers and Fathers' wisdom, many of us remain committed to the use of models, such as the transcendent approach, that help to inform the ongoing process of subjective understanding of the self-revealing God, and the trans-rational deep truths of Trinitarian theology. Rather than fear culture and difference, we are called to trust that God is very much present in our world and in our culture. The way we live this out will hopefully enable Christians to understand that there are diverse ways of expressing Christian discipleship in the world.

Trinitarian Presence in Places you Least Expect

At the time of writing the first version of this book, one of my dearest friends consistently challenged me about being too comfortably Christian. He is a self-confessed Unitarian who is on his own very particular Christian journey. He reminds me, like Peter Rollins, that if we are sincere about the transcendent God, and the apophatic tradition, then we need to ensure that we are not just attending to what we know and are comfortable with, but open to those things that are uncomfortable and disorientating, trusting

---

15 *Ibid.*, p. 37.

that God is in the mix somewhere. So when approaching the Bible, we don't just look at the bits we know we like to back up what we already think, but we attend to those bits that enrage and frustrate us. In a church I used to attend you would have been forgiven for thinking that the Bible consisted only of the New Testament, and that the letters of St Paul were really the only parts worth reading. It was all far too simplistic and comfortable. Part of the calling of new forms of church is not to run away from complex issues, but to live with a high regard for inclusive love and social and ecological justice. This is orthopraxis, so that life is not just about right thinking (orthodoxy) but about how this informs the way we live (orthopraxy).

This really hits home for me when we start talking about people I feel threatened by. To be very frank, this includes aggressive or abusive homeless people, alcoholics, racists, Islamic, Hindu, Jewish and Christian religious fundamentalists, those who demean women, and those who are homophobic. These are my top six hates. If I truly believe in this transcendent God of perichoresis, kenosis and panentheism, I need to be open to the possibility that this same God can be made present to such people. Can I trust God and be loving enough to make the Divine present to these people? Do I truly believe that God is seeking to draw all things into restored relationship with the Divine? Or to put it another way, do I believe that Christ, as the image (icon) of the invisible God, is self-revealed in all contexts, and beckons all people towards the Trinitarian God? This is hinted at strongly in Colossians:

He is the image [icon] of the invisible God, the firstborn of all creation. For by him all things were created: things in heaven and on earth, visible and invisible, whether thrones or powers or rulers or authorities; all things were created by him and for him. He is before all things, and in him all things hold together.

Colossians 1.15–17 (NIV)

This is profound and challenging stuff. As mentioned in Chapter 2, the Cappadocians utilize this idea of the image or icon of God to justify their argument of the three persons of God as the three images of God in one being. Scripture suggests that God illuminates the truth of God's nature through image. So how far is God illuminated in human experience outside of that which I feel comfortable with?

Following this text to its logical conclusion, should we not understand that all things encounter the Trinitarian nature of God, even fundamentalists and those from other faith traditions? Even those I would naturally seek to exclude? It was the insight of a shared transcendent experience that enabled the various Christian traditions of the charismatic renewal in the 1960s and 1970s to come together. They realized that God transcended difference through Holy Spirit-led, self-revealed activity. God challenges us in those profound places of difference and discomfort, unsettling us, encouraging us into encounter with the Divine that knows no bounds. This is one of the reasons the Moot Community (inspired by the Ikon community in Northern Ireland) went to a conservative Zionist Synagogue in Central London. We hoped to be transcendently challenged by the encounter. This book came out of that encounter.

So how is the Holy Trinity to be found present in surprising places? First, I was surprised to find strong Trinitarian understandings in some Christian fundamentalist writings. Haleblian outlines three doctrines considered basic to Christian orthodoxy, which he believes were in some way universally true for all people throughout all of history.[16] Even in this very black and white approach there is an acknowledgement that the Trinity 'articulates best what God is truly like and what faith in God means for life in the world'.[17] More controversially is the question, how is the Holy Trinity made present in other world religions?

---

16 K. Haleblian, 'The Problem of Contextualization', Missiology, XI, 1 (January, 1983), pp. 101–2.
17 Ibid.

Richard Sudworth reminds us, as the title of his new book suggests, that the Triune God is *Distinctly Welcoming*, and is present in our current twenty-first-century, multi-faith society. Even in the complexity of such a society, the God of the Trinity beckons:

> The concept of God's mission, not ours . . . should be no surprise to us . . . God is God and will move, by his Spirit, speaking to people, engineering encounters, listening to the cries and prayers of all sorts of odd outsiders in ways that God is completely at liberty to. This foundation of mission is, I believe, crucial to our understanding of other faiths. Once we see God, untamed, unconfined, working in and beyond the church, the way we approach and pray for others will inevitably shift.[18]

Sudworth's perspective is transcendent, believing that God's nature as Trinity, and the particular role of the Sustainer, means that the Trinity can be 'imaged' within any and all faiths, as God draws all to restored relationship with the Divine. Sudworth suggests that the belief in God as triune is core to the Christian faith. Therefore, God exists in community, and intends for us to live and work in relationship. As a result, a strong, caring community should be the focus and aim of the work we do. The desire to create community is therefore driven by the Triune God in us.[19] If this is true, then God is drawing all to experience the subjective truths the self-revealing God conveys. Sudworth again:

> In one sense, the concept of the Trinity underpins all the hallmarks of our distinctive faith. The Creator God is the Father, the Eternal Word and the Spirit. We understand God through the incarnation of his Son, and we in turn are called to incarnate the life of Christ through the Spirit. The redeeming nature of God is demonstrated in the cross where death is defeated and

---

18 R. Sudworth, *Distinctly Welcoming* (Bletchley: SCP, 2007), p. 29.
19 *Ibid.*, pp. 48–9.

where all humanity can turn to obtain new life in the Spirit. God's grace is manifest in the Son, full of grace and truth, and of the Spirit. We can trust in the resurrection of the dead and the newness of all things because the Father raised the Son from death and his Spirit is poured out on believers as a sign and promise of the new creation to come. God's covenant with us is established in the blood of the cross of his Son and sealed in us by the presence of the Spirit. Belief in a 'Triune God' is therefore something more than abstract and mystifying theology but the kernel of the Christian faith.[20]

Although Orthodox Judaism and Islam traditionally view the Greek Christian theological understanding of the Trinity as puzzling and even blasphemous, it is interesting that both these religions have mystical traditions that draw on an understanding of the Spirit and the immanence of God. Both Kabbalah in Judaism and Sufism in Islam resonate with the ideas of kenosis and panentheism – the idea of an immanent God, present in our world. Although they could never believe in a Triune God, they can believe in the One-God having the attributes of Creator, Redeemer and Companion.

Kabbalah draws heavily on the rabbinical form of the faith that emerged during the Babylonian exile. Yahweh had been seen as the transcendent Creator God, but after the exile and destruction of the temple, was seen as a God in their midst.[21] The very earliest passages of the Talmud describe God as being experienced through mysterious physical phenomena. The Rabbis spoke about the Holy Spirit, which had brooded over creation and the building of the sanctuary, making God's presence felt in a rushing wind or a blazing fire.[22] Kabbalists have traditionally understood that the Spirit makes God present through mystical, subjective experience.

20 *Ibid.*, pp. 71–2.
21 K. Armstrong, *A History of God* (London: Vintage, 1999), pp. 90–1.
22 *Ibid.*, p. 91.

While in exile, Jews held to the idea of the *Shekinah*, the glory of God. The word is derived from the Hebrew *shakan*, meaning 'to dwell with' or 'to pitch tent'. Therefore the Shekinah of God was mystically present with them wherever they were:

> The image of the Shekinah helped the exiles to cultivate a sense of God's presence wherever they were. The Rabbis spoke of the Shekinah skipping from one synagogue of the Diaspora to another; others said that it stood at the door of the synagogue, blessing each step that a Jew took on his way to the House of Studies . . .[23]

This mystically present God, related to Yahweh and the Holy Spirit, has remained a key concept in Kabbalah, the focus being the cultivation of a sense of God within each human being, so that dealings with others became sacred encounters.[24] If we believe that the Triune God becomes transcendently accessible to all things, including other faith traditions, we can understand this insight as the work of God. God, who is before all things, can be seen as drawing all to an understanding of the Trinity through the inspiration of the Holy Spirit.

Sufis believe that al-Lah is the absolute, and alone has true existence.[25] Rabiah, an early Sufi prophetess, wrote about al-Lah as a God of love who desires an intimate, redemptive relationship with all human beings.[26] Sufis hold a high view of God and Christ, professing that 'There is no god but al-Lah and Jesus is his Messenger.'[27] Al-Lah is seen as a sustaining presence in the universe. So again one could argue that the Triune God has transcendently brought these truths to the more mystical expressions of Islam.

---

23 *Ibid.*, p. 95.
24 *Ibid.*, p. 97.
25 *Ibid.*, p. 180.
26 *Ibid.*, pp. 265–7.
27 *Ibid.*

Both Sufism and Kabbalah emphasize a kenotic understanding of God, whereby love is poured out into all existence. This creative and salvific action reveals God's presence.[28] With such a focus on the love of God, God's sustaining presence in the world, kenosis and the Holy Spirit, there is plenty of common ground for fruitful dialogue between progressive Muslims, Christians and Jews.

I am not saying here that all religions lead to the same God. I am saying that God is mystically present to all things, and that we can have confidence that God is seeking to draw all things back into restored relationship with the Triune God, and that God will do what God will do. This transcendent and incarnational understanding of God's mission to the world requires us to take a more mystical and trusting approach. Mission and evangelism is not about us representing the absent God; it is much more about us trying to catch up with what God is already doing. Just as God used the charismatic renewal to bring deeper understanding of the Trinity to the Western Church, the mystical God uses the Holy Spirit to draw other religions to the truths of God, through subjective experience. Western Christianity must learn from that of the East, and begin to practise this more loving approach to the world's religions. Then maybe we will stop crusading against a perceived enemy, seeking instead to love people, hoping that they will encounter God through our actions and activities of hospitality and self-sacrifice. Here's hoping!

The Trinity has had a profound influence on the socio-political level also, challenging the status quo in South America for example. In the late 1960s to 1990s, understandings of the Trinity concerning social and ecological justice became keenly felt in places of significant poverty and oppression. Jürgen Moltmann, writing in 1967, and Leonardo Boff, in 1976, both draw on a relational model of the Trinity and the implications of perichoresis and panentheism to argue for the unity and relational connectedness of all things.[29]

---

28 *Ibid.*, p. 157.
29 L. Boff, *Liberating Grace* (Maryknoll, NY: Orbis Books, 1979).

ORTHOPRAXIS AND SACRAMENTALITY

Humanity should seek to incarnate the equality modelled within the Godhead on a societal level.[30] Liberation theologies stress Jesus' bias towards the poor and oppressed, and emphasize doing theology in specific social, political, and economic contexts. Jesus treated the poor preferentially, so this new theological methodology also gave priority to the poor. The idea of orthopraxis, or right action, came out of this commitment to practical love. Jesus wasn't merely a lovely person; he acted lovingly, challenged people, went to parties, and always included those who were poor or marginalized.

Further, out of this understanding of panentheism and Trinitarianism, Boff made significant advances when considering ecological justice. In the 1990s Boff sought, in a series of works on ecology, 'to connect the cry of the oppressed with the cry of the earth'.[31] In his understanding, an ecological liberation theology is a multi-dimensional project that seeks the welfare of people and the planet.[32]

Trinitarian theology radically challenges not only the Christian faith, but also other religions, and oppression and injustice throughout the world, even on the ecological level. It is quite awe-inspiring what has been made possible by the self-revealing God who, through the Holy Spirit, has given all things access to an experience of the transcendent, beckoning them into restored relationship.

Emerging Churches: Commitment to the Pursuit of Transcendent, Contextual Theology

An emphasis on transcendent encounter is prevalent within the Emerging Church, as is the practice of debate and dialogue as a method of exploration and knowledge acquisition. These are

___

30 J. Moltmann, *Theology of Hope: On the Ground and the Implications of a Christian Eschatology*, trans. James W. Leitch (London, SCM Press, 1967).
31 L. Boff, *Cry of the Poor, Cry of the Earth* (Maryknoll, NY: Orbis Books, 1997).
32 *Ibid.*

participative opportunities for people to explore, grapple with and seek meaning. Alternative worship is an interesting medium for seeking transcendence. Often alternative worship services have stations that act as opportunities for encounter, and for exploration of various concepts. This is all very much within the context of an active relationship with the transcendent God.

Much of the energy in the emerging church scene centres on energizing worship and reviving ancient practices, often seen as more genuine, raw and meaningful. The goal: a more 'biblical' church. Emerging worshippers value mystery, transcendence and the experience of communion.[33]

As explored earlier in Chapter 4, the Emerging Church has found a more ancient understanding of the idea of sacrament: the Spirit has made God present within each of us, so we are sacraments of God as we engage with the world. All life, by its very nature, is sacramental. This means that church, when understood as occurring in sacramental moments, happens whenever two or three people are gathered together. This may be over a pint of bitter at the local pub, whenever and wherever people pray together, or when people involve themselves in social justice. These expressions of sacramentality are moments when God can transcendently express the Divine in our lives. This refreshingly earthed understanding asserts that God is very present at all times and in all places. This is, after all, how I became a Christian in a nightclub, and how the Apostle Paul became a Christian travelling on a road.

Some alternative worship groups and emerging churches have been exploring the use of 'Godly Play' as a medium of worship and transcendent, Christian meaning-making. This is an approach to telling Bible stories that leaves room for participants to explore the story through the use of 'Wonderment Questioning'. This enables

---

33 http://www.religionlink.org/tip_060410.php – accessed 1.11.2011.

people to place themselves in the story and explore meaning that way. So rather than taking a Sunday-school approach of expecting people to know God through learning facts about God, it takes a transcendent, contextual approach that uses questioning to enable people to know God through transcendent experience. It is based on the ancient visual and oral art of storytelling, and brings awe, mystery and enchantment. To illustrate the power of this approach let me share an experience.

On a visit to a small emerging church group in New Zealand, I wanted to test out the power of Godly Play through doing it in a different culture. With the use of a sandpit and some basic props, I told some of the story of Abraham and Sarah, up to the point where they wander around the desert. I stopped telling the story near the end, to allow people to ask wonderment questions. Around the sandpit sat children with their parents, one of whom kicked off by saying, 'I wonder what it was like to hear God's voice?' I replied, 'I wonder?' After a little while, a girl no more than six years old said, 'I wonder what it is like to be a woman following a man who hears the voice of a God you cannot hear?' Again I replied, 'I wonder?' People were profoundly moved by this insight, which inspired all present to engage deeper with the meaning of the story. Later still, a small boy asked, 'I wonder what it is like to trust the voice of God enough to move out of town?' I replied, 'I wonder why you think Abraham had to trust God to move out of town?' To which he replied, 'I wonder if I would ever trust God enough to give up what I have?' The power in this approach for questing for spiritual meaning is self-evident. I am profoundly moved when I am involved in Godly Play. On this occasion I dutifully finished the story, people then painted what they had learnt, shared a snack meal and a prayer, and then left. If that is not profoundly inclusive and open-ended church, then I don't know what is.

Jerome Berryman, the creator of Godly Play, makes connections between the storytelling, wondering and responding of Godly Play with the ancient practice of *lectio divina*. This form of worship was developed by Christian monastic communities as a spiritual discipline of holy reading, meditation, prayer and responding to scriptural texts.[34] The reader comes to the text to seek an intuitive understanding, to grow in wisdom, to savour the aesthetic value of the words, and ultimately to encounter God, all of which is very similar to Godly Play. Godly Play therefore has strong similarities to pre-Enlightenment modes of thinking and knowing. It is not about objective data or the scientific method, which rejects subjective knowledge as myth and fantasy.[35] Rather it is about re-contextualizing the place of subjective experience as a way of knowing. God is made present via the Holy Spirit within the sacramental and transcendent moment. In my view, Taylor gives the best explanation for what is going on in Godly Play. In 2 Corinthians 3.16–18, we understand that when people turn to the Lord 'the veil is removed', which is freedom.[36] 'The Lord' of whom this passage speaks is the Holy Spirit, and the result of that clear vision of Jesus Christ is that we ourselves begin to be changed 'into the same image'[37] as Christ. The focus of the text is then thrown onto the end of verse 18, 'for this comes from the Lord, the Spirit'. As Taylor says, the relationship between the Holy Spirit and Christ is by now indistinguishable.[38] The Holy Spirit is dynamically involved in the gap between us, both as individuals and as communities, and God. Taylor has called the Holy Spirit the Go-Between God to reflect this. God the Holy Spirit is instrumental in the development of the 'I–Thou' relationship.[39] It is in this context that we understand the Holy Spirit as the counsellor that Jesus talked about, who would follow after him and guide Christians in all truth.[40]

---

34 J. W. Berryman, *The Complete Guide to Godly Play Volume 3* (Denver: Living the Good News Publishing, 2002), pp. 19, 21–22.

35 *Ibid.*, pp. 21–2.

36 NRSV.

37 Some translations state, more explicitly, 'into his likeness'.

38 J. V. Taylor, *The Go-Between God* (London: SCM Press, 1975), pp. 107–10.

39 *Ibid.*, p. 8.

40 John 14.15–27.

ORTHOPRAXIS AND SACRAMENTALITY

When drawn into relationship by the Triune God, our natural response is to try to connect with what we experience as an elusive presence.[41] We cannot fully capture our experience of God in any activity, story or rite, yet God's presence continually invites us to follow the glimpses disclosed through the Holy Spirit in sacramental moments.

The importance of Godly Play or *lectio divina* is the involvement of the Holy Spirit in these activities of worship. God the Spirit draws our attention to Christ, in whom alone the meaning of personhood is fully revealed. This drawing of our attention began at Pentecost and has continued to this day.[42] It is this openness to attention that enables Christians to know God through experience. As Taylor states:

> True attention is an involuntary self-surrender to the object of the attention . . . The Holy Spirit is that power which opens eyes that are closed, hearts that are unaware and minds that shrink from too much reality. If one is open towards God, one is open also to the beauty of the world.[43]

This sacramental understanding is ultimately expressed in table fellowship and the Eucharist, and it is profoundly exciting that so many emerging church groups have such a high regard for these practices. It has always amused me that the Moot Community's Eucharist services are generally the best attended. Their fusion of participation and contemplation with the ancient rite of the Eucharist truly brings transcendent experience. Such services are ancient:future places where God is free to do what God will do through the divine nature of kenotic love.

A commitment to transcendent spiritual pursuits implies a high regard to coming together as a community. Emerging churches

---

41 Berryman, *The Complete 1*, pp. 25–6.
42 Taylor, *The Go-Between*, pp. 107–17, 199.
43 *Ibid.*, pp. 18–19.

tend to see community as the reflection of God's nature, and it therefore receives significant emphasis. In the next chapter I will address the importance of the discovery of identity, both personal and communal, through the medium of intentional community.

Reflection

I have really pushed the boat out in this chapter, saying that what God models in perichoresis influences not only how we are church, but also our political, environmental and social circumstances. This takes us into new territory, territory often conceived of as off-limits by some Christians, and many fundamentalists in our own age. However, God empowers us with the ability and the insight to catch up with whatever God is up to in all spheres of human existence and social organization. Indeed, this now involves going beyond human existence itself, and reaching out to the whole of created matter. Without an understanding of the Trinity, it would be impossible to conceive of how it all relates in the transcendent power of God.

8

The Challenge of Human Community in a Culture of Individualism

New Year's Eve is often a time of taking stock of the year just passed, and giving consideration to or even making resolutions for the year ahead. It was in this spirit that, at a recent New Year's Eve party, someone asked me what I most longed for in life. As well as the usual wishes – partner, health and happiness – my friend was surprised to hear me say, 'and to live in a large enough house so I could set up an intentional spiritual community with close friends and others'. Ever since my student days, I have lived in accommodation that catered for multiple occupants, and I have always loved it. One of the strengths of emerging churches are the many students that, living in shared accommodation, help energize whatever is going on. From its inception, the Emerging Church movement in the UK has had a strong emphasis on community. As explored earlier, many in our contemporary culture crave relational intimacy in community, and yet fear it in equal measure.[1] This idealized desire for belonging in community goes very deep, but where does it come from? The reality of life in the twenty-first century is that it is largely an individualistic pursuit. In fact, we often assume that people are able to choose the communal life if they so desired, but I am not sure that this is really the case. Many of us have grown up in a culture of extreme individualism and independence, the secular mantra of our parents' generation. This

---

1 Z. Bauman, *Liquid Modernity* (Cambridge: Polity Press, 2000), pp. 100–6.

has resulted in many of us being rendered utterly under-skilled when it comes to communal life, which is about giving, taking and tolerance – particularly of those you do not like. In a culture of individualistic consumerism, doing and being community is quite a challenge. You can observe this lack of social skills when people are required to negotiate shared space, like public transport. Some have no idea about considering the needs of others, whether it be in queuing, in giving up a seat for a disabled or elderly person, getting on or off the bus, or listening to music (especially if you happen to have a loud speaker on your mobile phone!). The individual reigns supreme, and shows little regard to others. It is all about taking with no emphasis on giving.

In Chapter 6 I explored how many in today's culture define the self through patterns of consumption, which is in turn informed by information technology. Factors such as place, work and family are increasingly irrelevant in the formation of identity. Theologically, the challenge for community starts with a concern for what it means to be an individual human being. The biblical narrative of the 'covenanted being', which lies at the core of the Judaeo-Christian belief system, is quite different from the pick'n'mix, consumerist approach to personal identification. But what is this personal covenanted identity?

Covenant

A formal alliance or agreement initiated by God and formulated between God and a particular human community. This covenant gives identity to the group and individual human beings.

Such a covenant was created between Abram, Sarai and God (as Yahweh). This covenant brought about a change of names to demonstrate the deep connection between God and people, so both received an 'h' in their name of God – Abraham and Sarah. The focus of all biblical covenants is placed on grace (the unconditional love of God) and faith (openness to God, belief and experience of God).

> ## Life stage development
>
> Many psychologists have explored the developmental milestones that we proceed through from birth to childhood, adolescence, young adulthood, later adulthood and old age. From actual observation of people going through these stages, psychologists have suggested that in the transition between these life stages there can be good or unhealthy psychological outcomes.

Brueggemann draws on the concept of the 'covenanted self' to explore personal development from a biblical perspective.[2] He draws on the Psalms and the prophecy of Amos[3] to explore how the Israelites were covenanted to God's 'otherness'.[4] Brueggemann defines covenant as 'a theological commitment . . . to be enacted as a mode of shared life' and as 'a covenant commitment between God, individuals and groups of people.'[5] By implication personal identity is drawn from an understanding of the self in God. Brueggemann interprets this to be a radical alternative to our contextual post-secular 'consumption- informed identity', which he perceives as debilitating Christians and the Church.[6] He challenges the key psychological assumption of individualistic independence, in that from a Judaeo-Christian perspective the 'human-self' is never an isolated or autonomous being, but always and necessarily preceded by God's 'thou'.[7] Therefore the Christian assumption should be that God has evoked, summoned, authorized, and 'faithed' us into existence as persons. Brueggemann concurs with the psychological concept of life stage development because it connotes the sense of life as a journey

---

2 W. Bruggemann, *The Covenanted Self: Explorations in Law and Covenant* (Minneapolis: Fortress Press, 1999).

3 See Psalm 139.7–12; Amos 9.2–4.

4 Bruggemann, *Covenanted*, p. 2.

5 *Ibid.*, pp. 1, 37–9.

6 *Ibid.*, p. 1.

7 *Ibid.*, pp. 1–2.

of personal-identity formation. In this sense 'human beings' can be considered 'human becomings'.[8] Therefore, building a self-concept and world-view is less a matter of consumer choice, and more about engaging with God's otherness – the 'thou', which constantly inspires and undermines who we may choose to be. Spiritually understood, personal development is more of an enterprise of coming to terms with this 'other' or 'thou' in a way that is neither excessively submissive nor resistant. As with the Psalms, the presence of the other always reminds us that we are addressed, unsettled, unfinished, under way, and not fully who we intend or pretend to be. Brueggemann explores Winnicott's theory of emotional development, which addresses the consequences of maternal parenting on the child's life stage development.[9] Brueggemann interprets the outcomes of various life stages to and with a covenanted solution. For example, in early life the development of a healthy relationship between mother and child enables a dual capacity: to assert and to yield in the mother–child relationship. A healthy outcome would be a covenanting with intimacy. Covenanting is therefore a process, with God, with others and with the self.[10]

This process of the 'othering' of the self enables a covenanted identity to be formed that resources a healthy self-understanding in the context of others.[11] However, life remains an experience of ups and downs. Brueggemann draws on the Psalms to see how the Israelites coped with the struggle of survival in a chaotic and threatening world. His analysis of the Psalms reveals a pattern

---

8 *Ibid.*, pp. 3–6.

9 D. W. Winnicott, *The Maturational Processes and the Facilitating Environment: Studies in the Theory of Emotional Development* (London: Tavistock Press, 1971), as recorded in W. Bruggemann, *Covenanted*, pp. 3–6.

10 As Brueggemann details, with God – complaint and hymn, assertion of self and abandonment of self; with neighbours – joy and sorrow, truth in love, up-building in the midst of freedom; with the self – readiness to receive scattering and the freedom for gathering a self that is unlike the old one, a process of conversion and transformation. Brueggemann, *Covenanted*, p. 16.

11 Brueggemann draws on Psalm 103 to make this connection.

of orientation–disorientation–reorientation in response to various changes and crises.[12] In the midst of such constant change, individual identity relates to the process of the 'gathered-self' working through cyclical experiences of orientation, disorientation and reorientation; or, as Bauman would say, a process of dis-embedding and re-embedding. Lament Psalms express an appeal to God to make things right in a crisis. This is a full assertion of the self over God – 'Where are you God?' – followed sometimes by a faith that God 'will remain with us' even though times are difficult. Lament occurs in times of disorientation. The process works through to the sense of reorientation found in the Praise Psalms, where praise is the full abandonment of self to God. The experience of God in times of orientation, disorientation and reorientation, coupled with the experience of God through prayer, worship and teaching, all assist in the formation of self-identity covenanted to God's otherness. This process then continues in cycles of 'I–Thou' discovery. As Brueggemann states, God is a transcendent mystery that will not go away.[13] He sees the covenanted process as deeply embedding for individuals living in a threatening world. Such a process of identity formation is a radical alternative to the dis-embedding reality of our social context.

Volf reminds us that the 'I–Thou' relationship with God fully accommodates our uniqueness as individual human beings:

It is precisely the uniqueness of God's relation to me that makes me into a unique person. Yet in God's relation to me, a relation creating me as an individual human being, I do not stand as an individual isolated from other human beings and my environment. An isolated individual of this sort does not exist. Human beings are in actuality imbedded in a network of multiple and diverse social and natural relationships; this

---

12 Brueggemann, *Covenanted*, pp. 14–19.
13 *Ibid.*, p. 3.

applies not only to newborn infants, who have not yet become
subjects, but even to solitary ascetics, who do, after all, live a
spiritually real communion and must draw their sustenance
from nature . . . God's own relationship with human beings,
a relationship that first constitutes a human being into a person, always realizes itself through the differentiated existence
of every person in these multiple relations . . . Without other
human beings, even God cannot create a human being! Even if
God were to create an isolated being, that being would not be
a human being.[14]

Fascinatingly, Volf makes a connection with this and the wording
of the Genesis 1.27 text I looked at in Chapter 1:

This may be the anthropological significance of the peculiar
transition in Gen 1:27 from singular to plural: 'So God created
humankind in his image, in the image of God he created him;
male and female he created them.'[15]

By implication, our encounter with the Trinity is as unique human
individuals. It is the Creator who leads the perichoresis and mysteriously institutes us as unique human beings, and it is the participation of the Redeemer through the Spirit in co-operation with
human community that constitutes us as human beings. People
then have the freedom to either realize this connection with God
and human community, or to reject it. This sense of constitution
goes even deeper with all those who have chosen to realize the
Christian faith as their story.

Here in our personal interiority we find deep connection with
the Holy Spirit – the unfathomable mystery of God's indwelling –
informing our self-identity.[16] Volf goes further, suggesting that it

---

14 M. Volf, *After Our Likeness: The Church as the Image of the Trinity*
(Cambridge: Eerdmans, 1998), pp. 182–3.

15 *Ibid.*, p. 183.

16 *Ibid.*, p. 188.

is Christ who, recognizing our individual uniqueness, draws us together to realize our common-unity.

The Spirit present in all Christians 'opens' each of them to all others. It starts them on the way to creative mutual giving and receiving, in which each grows in her or his unique way and all have joy in one another.[17]

Here we see the importance of the inter-relatedness of God, the individual person and community. Throughout this book I have explored the implications of perichoresis, the interpenetration of the three persons of the Godhead, which goes far beyond what we can conceive. I have explored how church that is modelled on the Trinity lives through the participation of its members, who are themselves constituted by the Holy Spirit. The Triune God, who through the Holy Spirit is made present, interpenetrates each of us as unique human beings. Therefore community becomes an important environment for the realization of our unique potential. The place of the Church, as the alternative, loving and inclusive community reflecting the invisible Kingdom of God, then becomes the highest expression of this community, which loves people into their potential. The place of community is key.

It is unsurprising then to find that if the constituting effects of community that enable the individual to fully develop are not present or are disrupted, the individual is unable to realize the fullness of their potential. As I explored in my first book, and more briefly in the previous chapter, our post-industrial Western society is characterized by fluidity, and the hugely significant shift from communities built around 'place' to those of 'network'. As a result of the fluidity of network communities, relationships are constantly changing, particularly in urban areas. In this context it becomes extremely difficult to be constituted as a human being, to realize your potential. As social relationships are dramatically

---

17 *Ibid.*, p. 189.

affected by consumption, married and unmarried relationships cease to be 'for ever', and tend to be determined more by perceived happiness and personal fulfilment. In the UK, we have not recovered from the way community was threatened and even despised in the late 1970s and 1980s. This attitude was epitomized by the then Prime Minister Margaret Thatcher, who said:

> There's no such thing as society. There are individual men and women and there are families. And no government can do anything except through people, and people must look after themselves first.[18]

For quite a while in the UK, the idea of community has been neglected in favour of a self-centred personal responsibility. At the same time the UK has become one of the largest economic centres of the world, but has also consistently been one of the worst countries with regard to poverty and child deprivation. There is also an increasingly unethical gap between the incomes of richest and poorest in the country. In a culture centred on the individual, there has been significant neglect at a community level.

Currently, many of the UK's urban contexts suffer from problems associated with the absence of parents, particularly fathers, in a culture of ever-increasing under-age sex and teen parenthood. Young people are under enormous pressure in our newly highly sexualized culture. It is no surprise, then, that the post-industrial, postmodern West has seen an exponential rise in suicides, mental illness, homelessness, relationship breakdown and stress.

As explored in the previous chapter, there is a huge desire for deeper forms of personal identity, a hunger for inner peace and happiness. Many have such a poor sense of personal identity that they don't realize their need for God. The Church as *ekklesia*, the alternative community, a visible and yet incomplete sign of God's Kingdom, must enable people to achieve their potential as

---

18 http://en.wikiquote.org/wiki/Margaret_Thatcher – accessed1/11/2011.

'human becomings' through the constituting effects of community and covenant with God. So how is this possible?

The sense of community in many Emerging and Fresh Expressions of church is very strong, with a commitment to support, encouragement and mutual learning. In my research of Emerging and Fresh Expressions, it is evident that many of these projects encounter people who are spiritual tourists, seeking spiritual meaning and community. This questing leads people to check out these communities, sometimes staying on the edge of events for one to two years before getting fully involved. With an emphasis on 'belonging before believing', many look to the Emerging Church for the opportunity to explore their identity and their need for God. It is unsurprising that many emerging churches draw heavily on the wisdom of pastoral carers, spiritual directors, mental health workers, psychiatrists, social workers, therapists and psychologists. All these assist emerging churches to achieve communities of health and wellbeing. Committed friendships are built up; we learn to open up about our lives and struggles, often learning from the experience of others. Most importantly, community is an opportunity to learn how to tolerate people who are different or challenging. It also aids in the patterning of one's life, so as to be able to turn up reliably at events. We learn to trust, to listen, to give, and in short to reach our potential. In this way, the Trinitarian God, through the constitution of identity, strengthens incomplete church communities, enabling us to model the beauty of perichoresis, and therefore human becoming in community. The similarities between these forms of church and 'therapeutic communities' are significant.[19] Both have regular community governance meetings that promote ownership of the community. Tasks are shared, and new people are supported and socialized into the community. Leadership is flat and modelled as servanthood and participation. In this way participants have their uniqueness as individuals affirmed and begin to realize their potential. And of course,

---

19 http://en.wikipedia.org/wiki/Therapeutic_community – accessed 1/11/2011.

community inculcates an awareness of others who must also be encouraged in the same way. This is after all the strength of the mystical communion model I identified in Chapter 4. A whole life approach to discipleship and catechesis is also essential. The Beta Course and Soul Sparks are two very good examples of this.[20]

It is important that the Church realizes that people no longer come fully skilled and able to engage with community. Many carry unresolved psychological and social issues; many are struggling with stress, anxiety and depression. Many are confused about who they are, or carry deep issues of personal doubt or self-loathing. All of this will be projected into the life, relationships, hopes and dreams of the spiritual community they attend, if not dealt with adaptively. This is why so many churches are terribly dysfunctional. Our hope has to be that if we really face up to these difficulties, they can be addressed and we can have healthy, adaptive co-journeying communities.

The Moot Community, of which I am part, has promoted the use of external spiritual directors, mentors and counsellors, and is now considering running a stress and contemplative prayer course, soon to be trialled. We seek to emulate the complexity of the perichoretic Triune Godhead by recognizing the interconnectedness of personal identity, health, church and spirituality. Any attempt to do church must offer places for people to find themselves, to learn life skills and find health, as well as explore the narratives of the Christian faith. One key asset in this endeavour is the place of contemplative prayer. Generally speaking, a form of spirituality that is cognitively 'true' is of less importance than one that 'works'. Many are willing to try anything if there's a chance it will bring stillness, peace and centredness to the stress and restlessness experienced in everyday life. The ancient Christian contemplative tradition is the perfect resource for meeting the very real, personal needs of today. I witnessed the potency of this

---

20 http://www.soulspark.org.uk/SoulSpark/Soul_Spark.html – http://www.beta-course.org/ – accessed 10.11.2011.

contemplative approach at the Mind, Body and Spirit Festival stall mentioned earlier. Here, short introductory approaches to contemplative prayer opened up whole vistas of opportunity for those spiritual tourists who tried it. Some found centredness, peace and experiences of authentic transcendence, through an openness to spiritual encounter. Others cried in relief at getting beyond pain; others expressed joy at getting beyond restlessness. It is my hope that these people continued using these effective contemplative approaches to Christianity.

It is not just alternative worship groups, and Emerging and Fresh Expressions of church, who have found this approach to work: it has also been effective in the corporate business world:

Corporate executives seek opportunities for silent retreats. Major businesses add meditation rooms to the workplace environment. Women and men earning impressive salaries quit their jobs to find a quieter pace, a more peaceful environment, a closer connection with the land, a greater sense of purpose.[21]

In her profound essay 'Spirituality in a Postmodern Era', Marie McCarthy identifies contemplative awareness as essential to the development of authentic spirituality. In her view, authentic spirituality is that which 'works', in that it makes connections with the restless, searching nature of spiritual tourists.

Authentic spirituality is grounded in the discipline of contemplative awareness. Awareness as a discipline opens us to levels of reality not immediately apparent. It enables us to see ourselves, our circumstances, our world without illusion . . . It requires stillness, receptivity, and availability. The discipline of awareness involves deep listening, which is marked by waiting,

---

21 M. McCarthy, 'Spirituality in a Postmodern Era', in J. Woodward and S. Pattison (eds), *The Blackwell Reader in Pastoral and Practical Theology* (Oxford: Blackwell, 2000), pp. 193–4.

attending, and presence. We must sit in the stillness, wait, and listen deeply. And we must be silent. The discipline of contemplative awareness is nurtured in the practice of silence. We consciously create pools of silence in which to hear. We quiet the many voices around us and within us as we wait to hear a word of revelation . . . Contemplative awareness does not lead to withdrawal from the world, but a deep immersion in the world. One becomes more aware of and attentive to the realms of everyday life, to the joys and sorrows, the sufferings and ecstasies, the struggles and triumphs of very real people in very real circumstances . . . Authentic spirituality, then, is marked by dynamic relationship between contemplation and action which works toward the healing of the world and wellbeing of all creation.[22]

This extremely ancient approach to prayer and contemplation provides an opportunity for the meeting of God and humans, through the power of the imagination. It is part of a long tradition that dates from the early Christian mystics, through to the contemplatives and charismatics of today. However, the practices involved in contemplative prayer aren't known as disciplines for nothing – they require application and diligence. In our culture of instant gratification, learning this is going to be hard work. However, one can learn simple techniques that gradually equip the user to then go deeper. The Moot Community now aim to include contemplative approaches to prayer in most services, and take the opportunity to conduct workshops and seminars on a regular basis. Something that must be borne in mind when developing the contemplative prayer life is that a balance must be struck between being alone and being in community. It can become an overly individualistic pursuit, with the result that we shy away from community. As we have already seen, such a situation makes it very difficult to realize our potential. McCarthy again puts this better than I can:

22 *Ibid.*, pp. 199–200.

Grounding in a community of discourse, belief, and practice is a further feature of authentic spirituality. We do not undertake the spiritual quest alone. We need communities which nurture and hold us, communities which keep traditions and charisms alive and which hand them on to the next generation. Because we are human beings, we most often come to an encounter with the sacred through the mediation of the traditions, practices, and charisms of particular spiritual traditions. And these traditions and charisms take root, develop, and are handed on only in the context of a community that keeps them alive. Thus an individual, privatized, or purely personal spirituality is an oxymoron. Authentic spirituality can never be an isolated, privatized, individual affair. It is always located in a particular community from which it derives flavour, character and efficacy.[23]

So the place of community, and covenanted relationship with God and others, is crucial in our human 'becomingness'. It is in the *communion* of differing stories, the stories of God, the stories of other people, that we find our voice and our own unique story. A large proportion of people in emerging churches have come from pretty extreme fundamentalist expressions of faith. Many are therefore very cynical about prayer and the Bible, largely because they have experienced abuses of both. It is therefore crucial for emerging churches to provide the opportunity for deeper expressions of prayer, and a re-engagement with the Bible, which for some is really difficult.

It is important here to grasp the role of the Church as an 'interpretative community'.[24] Within the intimacy of relationship, various truths and interpretations can be discussed and owned by the community. Although the Bible was inspired by God it

---

23 *Ibid.*, p. 200.
24 Attributed to Stanley Hauerwas in P. Janowiak, *The Holy Preaching: The Sacramentality of the Word in the Liturgical Assembly* (Collegeville, MN: Liturgical Press, 2000), p. 151.

was written by human beings and is therefore not without inconsistency. Comprehension of the Bible requires the use of human sense organs and the mind. While this may at times be a God-inspired activity, it is also very human. The power of interpretative communities is their ability to balance reason with experience and understanding, so that the Holy Spirit can promote a shared understanding. Being utterly counter-fundamentalist and non-dualistic, this approach enables people to hold onto their own thoughts and understanding. It enables ongoing dialogue, and the sense that knowledge continually unfolds through transcendent encounter. New thinking that emerges as communities explore their tradition can be tested against established thought. Shared language and world-view are constructed socially, as a subjective, shared attempt to express meaning about God and existence. This shared narrative then becomes the narrative of the individual. Openness to new meaning is very healthy if it remains in the context of the ongoing tradition. This is not so easy in groups that do not have a deep understanding of tradition, and the danger of throwing the baby out with the bathwater becomes acute. Many emerging churches have weekly groups that operate as interpretative forums, encouraging learning through discussion and experience – also yet another form of transcendent encounter. Group consensus acts as a healthy reality check of the truth of what is being said.

Being this type of church is far from easy. There is a real danger that powerful, charismatic characters will manipulate meaning and subvert the community. Real, transparent and agreed governance structures are important to prevent such abuses. Such forms of church do not work if numbers rise to the point where meetings become impersonal. I don't think you can do this form of church in numbers greater than 120, and around half this number is preferable. If an interpretative community is going to draw effectively on contemplative spirituality, there needs to be a high regard to openness, discernment and action. Openness should be characterized by active and respectful listening to the views of others, and by a sense of humility when before the unfamiliar, the new and the unexpected.[25] This form of discernment, says McCarthy:

> Invites us to put our lives in dialogue with the tradition through prayer, reflection, meditation, individual and group guidance, and other practices. They encourage attentive listening and awareness of how we are being called and where we are being led . . . looking for certain signs such as a sense of inner and outer freedom, an awareness of the connectedness and inter-relation of all creation, a rootedness in tradition coupled with openness to the new, and a sense of deep inner peace.[26]

> [Such discernment] can help us to retrieve the role of community in nurturing a deep spiritual life. It can provide the means for examining and critiquing both ancient and contemporary forms of community living and it can assist us in reconstructing forms of community life which are real and effective in today's society.[27]

While these forms of spiritual community are demanding, the rewards are great when we get it right. There are tools that can assist us in this pursuit. First, as discussed previously there is real power in the formulation of a rhythm of life to help develop the interpretative dimension of the community. The pattern of spirituality discussed in this chapter resonates with the foundational vision of many monastic and new monastic movements. The Moot Community's Rhythm of Life has helped us develop our own sense of the narrative of the Christian tradition of which we are a part. The practice of hospitality is vital, particularly for engaging with people who have had no church experience. From my own experience, unconditional hospitality has been the key

---

25 *Ibid.*, pp. 200–1.
26 *Ibid.*, p. 201.
27 *Ibid.*, p. 204.

to enabling this way of being church to happen. I am still foster-
ing friendships with spiritual tourists who have surfed the edges
of Moot since its inception. However, the rewards of hospitality cannot be reaped overnight; it takes years' worth of commitment. My friend Michael Volland literally walked around
Gloucester for several months, talking to people in all sorts of
places, miles away from the Church, with a view to building an
incarnational expression of church. A transcendent model of
contextual theology enables us to trust God to be present as we
are attentive to the conversations and meetings we have in the
ordinariness of life. A new missional community called Feig grew
out of Michael's relational connections with people in central
Gloucester.

After all, this is the form of church that helped form me into
the person and Christian I am today. The self-confidence I gained
helped me believe I could be an occupational therapist and eventually, staggeringly, an Anglican priest. These forms of church
have been crucial in my own walk through life.

However, human becoming through community is not just
about contemplation, participation and worship. There are also
real opportunities for practical action. This is connected with the
very real need for churches to consider commitment to place as
well as network. Some examples of practical action are those who
work with the homeless, who set up cafés to connect with local
people in public spaces, those who are involved in social care.
After all, the source of our inspiration, the monks and friars of
the pre-modern period, were very involved in practical projects
with the poor and needy. I suggest that all Christian communities need to consider how they can practically serve their local
communities – both of place and network – with a commitment to being present to ordinary people through loving service.
Personally I love the idea that the church's café becomes the hub
of the local community. A number of emerging churches have
done precisely this, and their communities have become profound places of inclusion, love and service. A community taking

on such a project, with a degree of maturity in contemplative prayer, can really enable growth through giving rather than taking and consumption.

In a world of so much need, there is only so much our communities can sustain before they fall into the trap of attempting, and inevitably failing, to fulfil the role of social services. Nevertheless, there are real opportunities for engagement and an openness to doing through 'contemplative-action' is an important place to start. We need to remember that when our communities reflect the love and acceptance of the Triune God they can truly become places of transformation and growth. No one expresses this better than Jean Vanier, whose whole life is centred on developing community as a profound expression of becoming and healing. He supports adults with learning difficulties whose experience of rejection and loss of identity has been internalized in quite extreme ways. In his community these individuals became connected and experience belonging, love and forgiveness. This leads to transformation (human becoming) as they follow the example modelled by Christ, and the Trinity more generally.

This sounds good in theory, but how does one practically do this type of Christian community? For Jean Vanier, it begins with following the Trinitarian God of creative love:

> To the poverty of our human minds the possibility of a destiny conceived by God, and freedom, seem contradictory. Yet it is not so. For the wisdom of God and God's respect for each person is so great, that a destiny of ultimate fulfilment, and individual freedom, are gently married, and the glory of God and of creation flows from this union. God has the secret of loving us to freedom, inviting us to share in the creativity of love. Because so many of us have experienced a love coming from parents – or others – that is stifling or crippling or possessive, it is difficult to believe we are loved by a love that brings us to freedom, and that God's plan goes far beyond the wonder and beauty of the creation we know . . . Yes the deepest song of everything in

creation reflects the unity of the Trinity: three persons poured out in love for one another.[28]

The starting place of community is the willingness to work at the task, to believe that a group of acquaintances can become community. As we follow Christ,[29] the community eventually becomes more inter-related, and so reflects God's perichoretic nature. Christ expressed this in how he lived and related to others, starting with the disciples. The challenge is now for us Christians and the Church to live this way, reflecting this 'becoming' in our communities as we follow the example modelled by the Trinitarian God.

The Becoming of Community

One of today's greatest myths is that personal fulfilment has to do with pleasure or happiness, and conversely that pain has nothing to do with authentic living.

So many of us flee from people crying out in pain, people who are broken. We hide in a world of distraction and pleasure or in 'things to do' . . . Or if we do not flee from suffering perhaps we revolt in anger. Many people who appear powerful and successful can also feel worthless deep inside themselves. They have money, power, education, status, but they lack what is essential: a heart that is free and loving, the knowledge that they are loved. They seem unable to relate, and feel broken and empty inside . . . They too feel they belong to no one. They feel that terrible pain of being unable to love, of isolation, unable to break out of their shell to relate with trust and faithfulness, in communion with others.[30]

---

28 J. Vanier, *The Broken Body* (London: DLT, 1988), pp. 26–8.
29 *Ibid.*, pp. 26–62.
30 *Ibid.*, pp. 1, 13.

A starting place for Christian community is the dispelling of the myth that pain and suffering have nothing to do with the human journey of becoming. Generally speaking, pain and suffering is made worse by isolation and exclusion. There is nothing more powerful than sharing one's pain in community, and finding support and care. Somehow, knowing that we are cared for, and that our carers suffer similarly, makes our pain more bearable. Further, being connected with others who are also in pain helps us develop adaptive coping strategies. This is fairly obvious stuff; after all it is the basis of the hugely successful twelve-step programme. Such groups meet regularly for mutual support and to develop coping strategies, with appeal to a higher power. Both Vanier and the followers of twelve-step programmes have discovered the power of spiritual community. A community that is steeped in the Christian narrative, and that draws inspiration from the perichoretic relationships of the Trinity, can be hugely transformative.

> In the beauty and fragility of this experience [of community] lies also its pain. In awakening our capacity to love, it awakens what is deepest in us which includes our vulnerability and sensitivity . . . Community provides the necessary safeguards and limits but also the support to allow us to live fully these experiences of joy and pain. Community gives the confirmation we need to remain faithful. It can provide also the challenge we need to go forward, so that we can live these experiences as times of growth on our pilgrimage, which is both a journey to greater wisdom and to the deeper rooting of our being.[31]

However, maintaining a healthy community when many of its members are in pain must be carefully managed, so as to promote healthy inter-dependency and not co-dependency. This is why twelve-step groups must have skilled facilitators. In the context

---

31 *Ibid.*, pp. 94–6.

of community, this can be self-regulating, where regular discussions are governed by agreed ground rules aimed at building trust and openness. An effective community must be grounded in a commitment to openness and the sharing of love and support in the midst of deep pain.

The Becoming of Belonging

The achievement of openness and honesty are important milestones in the growth of any community. However, many flounder in the attempt to establish the vital sense of trust and belonging:

> The Christian churches seem to many people irrelevant, for they too are more a cause of division and of war than a source of unity and peace.[32]

Churches need to rediscover how to become inclusive communities that inspire people to go deeper with the Trinitarian God. Communities that encourage trust and belonging can become transformative communities:

> The sense of belonging flows from trust: trust is the gradual acceptance of others as they are with their gifts and their limits, each one with the call of Jesus. And this leads to the realization that the body of community is not perfectly whole and cannot be, that this is our human condition. And it is all right for us to be less than perfect. We must not weep over our imperfections. We are not judged for being defective. Our God knows that in so many ways we are lame and half-blind . . . but we can walk together in hope, celebrating that we are loved in our brokenness.[33]

---

32 *Ibid.*, p. 15.
33 *Ibid.*, pp. 98–9.

A truly open community is one where those who do not believe can participate and belong, alongside those who do. This can be a challenge, but it is very much within our grasp. Many Emerging and Fresh Expressions of church are committed to this, knowing that people often need to work out who they are in a safe place, before they realize their need for God. The temptation in this context is to dilute the Christ-centredness of the group, but quite the opposite is required if people are to have a positive experience of Christian community. Building such communities is really tough, and takes a long time, but once established the rewards are substantial.

The Becoming of Forgiveness

Community at its most basic form is about the sense of common-unity or 'at-one-ment'. If unity is to be maintained, there must be a commitment to forgiveness. This is particularly difficult in communities that are characterized by a diversity of behaviour and values, as emerging churches often are. Additionally, our wider culture is not good at forgiveness. When public figures are disgraced, there is very little sense of redemption. No community centred on love, trust and belonging can be maintained without a commitment to forgiveness. Now this is not a green light for aggressive or dehumanizing behaviour, but rather an acceptance that we are incomplete and will make mistakes. A healthy discipline worth considering for individuals committed to Christian community is external spiritual direction or mentoring. Awareness of self (strengths and weaknesses) is vital in negotiating a healthy spiritual community. Otherwise, our emotional brokenness will always be projected into the community. Forgiveness is the choice to let go, to rise above, and to choose approaches centred on meditation and finding the common good. Where this is modelled it can lead to profound community:

> Forgiveness is the source and the rock of those who share their lives: to forgive each day, to forgive and forgive and forgive,

149

and to be forgiven just as many times . . . Forgiveness is the ce-
ment that bonds us together: it is the source of unity; it is the
quality of love; that draws togetherness out of separation . . .
Forgiveness is letting go of unrealistic expectations of others
and of the desire that they be other than they are. Forgiveness is
liberating others to be themselves, not making them feel guilty
for what may have been . . . Forgiveness is to follow Jesus, to be
like him, for he came to give and forgive, to take from the shoul-
ders of people the yoke of guilt that locks them into a prison of
sadness and sterility, and prevents them from flowing and living
freely.[34]

Forgiveness is so profoundly counter-cultural and uncommon
that it must be learnt. Therefore it must firstly be modelled in
community. One cannot assume that the ability to forgive follows directly from the intellectual comprehension of it. Feelings
go deep, and rising above our own pain and insecurity is one of the
greatest challenges facing us as human becomings. Often, communities that have initially established trust, belonging and love
fail because of division created by a lack of forgiveness. So the ability to forgive flows from a resourcing contemplative spiritual life
sustained in the unconditional love of God. Then people can truly
forgive when it hurts.

The Becoming of Hope

When a community practises love, openness to joy and pain, belonging and forgiveness, it becomes a profoundly hopeful place –
an unfortunately rare phenomenon in our world today:

Helping each other, growing in trust, living in thanksgiving,
learning to forgive, opening up to others, welcoming them, and

---

34 *Ibid.*, pp. 106–7.

striving to bring peace and hope to our world. So it is that we come to put down roots in community – not because it is perfect and wonderful, but because we believe that Jesus called us together. It is where we belong and are called to grow and to serve.[35]

A community that is able to live this way, no matter how imperfectly, has a lot to give to the world. When coupled with a healthy, culturally relevant expression of worship, mission and community, it can be a potent expression of deep Christian faith. Unfortunately such hope-driven Christian communities are rare, a factor that I believe relates directly to the state of decline the Church now finds itself in.

The Becoming of Justice

Once people find hope, forgiveness, openness, belonging and community, it is hoped that they will have had personal experience of the love of God. This may take a long time, but often, as God's story and the community's story become the individual's story, there is a shift from consumption to production, from taking to giving. Some experience God through loving acts of service, others through spiritual encounters. Regardless of which medium it is, the justice and inclusion experienced in the perichoretic community inevitably becomes the model to follow. In this way, our communities become characterized by justice, peace, and ministry to the poor, excluded or oppressed. We can then be thought of as being in our culture but not of it. The Emerging Church is one of a number of recent innovations in the Church that has social, economic and ecological justice as foundational values. Justice and mercy are deeply humanizing forces in our world, where thinking globally and acting locally can have a significant impact. This

---

35 *Ibid.*, p. 99.

is not an easy journey – Christ, many saints of the Church, and plenty of modern-day figures, such as Martin Luther King Junior, were killed for similar values. As Eberhard Arnold said:

> We must live in community because we take our stand in the spiritual fight on the side of all those who fight for freedom, unity, peace, and social justice . . . Yet we are not the driving force in this – it is we who have been driven and who must be urged on.[36]

If church communities desire to become places of love, belonging, forgiveness, hope and justice, they will follow the values of the perichoretic Godhead. The missional and evangelistic impact of a church modelled on the very becoming of God could be enormous.

Reflection

Two years ago I was taken to Margate, Kent, to experience an interesting Anglican church that was a cross between a charismatic evangelical and a fresh expression of church. I was very cynical and did not want to go. However, I was shocked by the challenge I encountered. The church was situated in a deprived area of Margate that had become a ghetto for drug addicts, young offenders and asylum seekers. Stories from a recent baptism service conducted by those living in local temporary accommodation were deeply moving. God had met with them in profound ways in the midst of their pain, giving many the impetus needed to sort their lives out. Whole families, separated through legal proceedings, crime and other factors, came together and celebrated in the joy of the moment, before they were separated and returned to various custodial places. The depth of relationship spoke of a very real sense

---

36 E. Arnold, *We Live in Community* (Robertsbridge, East Sussex: Plough Publishing House, 1995), pp. 5, 30.

of loving commitment in that community. In the brief moments of the worship service, the church had enabled those present to experience a transcendent encounter with God. It was hoped that these very real encounters would encourage many to seek God's help in facing the darker side of their lives. I was truly humbled by the experience. Thinking about it afterwards, I realized that this is the power of a church that chooses to reflect the Triune God in what it does and says. The next challenge for that church is how it can maintain such a ministry and participative community. We also face the same challenge: are we prepared to live this costly way in our post-secular context? To understand how we sustain this giving out of love to the world, we next need to explore how the Trinitarian God's nature is characterized by mission.

9

Mission as Participation in God

At a lecture I attended in Cambridge, I was struck by the passion of a Greek Orthodox priest as he talked about how God's pericho-retic love is expressed in God's mission. He spoke of God being like three people holding hands in a dynamic dance. God's love is shared in deep connection and divine fun, and God then expresses this love to the world by inviting human beings to join in with the dance. In this understanding, mission – *missio Dei,* the mission of God – is not some form of aggressive divine marketing strategy, a way of getting more people in church and consuming religion. No, the essence of God's mission is not primarily concerned with getting more bums on seats, nor chalking up conversions for that matter; rather, God's mission is expressed in transformative, self-giving love:

> Mission has its origins in the heart of God. God is a fountain of sending love. This is the deepest source of mission. It is im-possible to penetrate deeper still; there is mission because God loves people.[1]

The history of the Church in mission has not consistently held to this high view of loving inspiration. Unfortunately mission, po-litical colonialization and the domination of the Western progress-myth have historically been deeply connected to Western Christian

---

1 D. J. Bosch, *Transforming Mission: Paradigm Shifts in Theology of Mission* (New York: Orbis Books, 1991), p. 392.

154

expansionism. In this understanding mission was about sending Christian missionaries abroad for evangelism, and to establish Western modes of civilization, replacing pre-modern forms of culture and human society. As discussed in previous chapters concerning contextual theology and Christendom, there is a great danger that this form of mission and evangelism is about power over people in a vision of 'unity in conformity'. I have certainly had negative experiences of this form of evangelism and mission in the UK, which can be disrespectful, aggressive and dualistic.

So what does mission look like when it seeks to affirm a Trinitarian-inspired understanding of the Church with a transcendent model of contextual theology, inspired by a loving engagement with the world?

So far in this book we have focused on a Trinitarian understanding of faith as the gathering of a loving, participative and justice-orientated community reflecting the nature of God – but this is only part of the story. We need to look to the story of salvation history to understand the bigger picture. God's divine nature demonstrates this gathering, but it is followed by sending. At the point of creation, we encounter a God expressing love to the cosmos; God creating the cosmos out of love for created matter. At the point of the incarnation of God the Redeemer, we encounter Jesus coming in human form, the mystery of God the Son being sent into the world to live among people as a person. Jesus is sent as a human becoming to outwork the purposes of God as a paradox – wholly God and wholly human. At the point after the resurrection the Trinity is re-gathered, and then God the Holy Spirit is sent to be the perfect Counsellor and Sustainer for the Church until the consummation of all things, when God draws all things back into restored relationship at the end of time. So the story of God is centred on the rhythm of gathering of the divine persons in love, participation and justice and then the sending of divine persons to express this love, participation and justice to the cosmos and humanity. This gathering and sending has something to say about the nature of church as the body of Christ, which is to share in this divine nature of gathering and sending.

The biblical idea of the apostles is that those who were gathered were also to be sent. The New Testament Greek word here is *apostolos*, meaning 'one who is sent forth as a messenger'. We see this gathering and sending expressed in the persons of God, and we see it expressed in Christ's gathered community of the disciples who became the sent apostles. So the *missio Dei* becomes the *missio Christi*, which in turn becomes the *missio Ecclesiae* (mission of the Church). We then, as participants of the Church, are sent out to be apostles ourselves – to express self-giving love to people and to creation.

> The church community, participating in God's life, is God's special people living God's life of communion in a covenant of relation and love, a people convinced of its fundamental equality through its common baptism in the name of the Triune God. But as communion-in-mission, this image takes on a dynamic meaning as God's people in pilgrimage . . . committed to sharing the full implications of God's covenant with all humanity.[2]

This sharing of the full nature of God is good news for all people and for the whole cosmos. This expands on the meaning of *apostolos,* with the Church being a messenger, where the message is one of good news: in ancient Greek, the word *evangelium*, from which we derive the word evangelism. So mission is fully expressed in loving activity, both evangelism (sharing the good news) and action (seeking economic, social and ecological justice).

Mission, then, is not what many Christians have understood it to be. It is not about standing up for a missing God in a godless world, with all the horrendous power play that this approach

---

2 S. B. Bevans and R. P. Schroeder, *Constants in Context* (New York: Orbis Books, 2008), p. 299.

creates. Quite the opposite: mission is about catching up with what God, who remains radically present to all life and created matter, is already doing.

This understanding of mission must start with listening and being attentive to God. Churches committed to mission need to start in contemplative prayer, before seeking to begin mission activity as 'contemplative-action'. Mission begins from a deep relational communion in God – the prayerful participation with God and with the church community:

> The church is understood as a communion; it is a people made one with the unity of the Father, the Son and the Holy Spirit . . . What the church is in its deepest reality, it is called to be in its every aspect. The building of a vibrant community life, therefore, where real sharing, mutuality, justice, and solidarity take place.[3]

The call to the Church is to express its abundant life in deep humanity and flourishing community, and then express this to the world. This requires a profound depth of relational community in order to balance communal self-care with self-giving.

In a more Trinitarian theology, evangelism is inspired by Jesus, in the power of the Spirit, who entered into dialogue with all sorts of people. In fact we encounter Jesus munching his way throughout the Gospels with all sort of outsiders and inadequates, in loving and caring conversation. In these moments we see Jesus expressing the good news of God, and enacting radical social and economic justice by consorting with precisely the sorts of people he was supposed to avoid in order to keep pure.

Many Emerging and Fresh Expressions of church are inspired by this interpretation of Jesus' actions, and have set up many new forms of evangelism by running a variety of pub and café discussion groups. The hope is that these are about loving discourse, which

---

3 *Ibid.*, p. 298.

God the Holy Spirit will use for the Kingdom, rather than about filling people's heads with clever facts as some form of manipulative power play. Evangelism begins with the forming of loving relationships with those who are not Christian, to build trust, and the desire to share personal experience of this loving God. As discussed earlier, new monasticism has taken this further – a form of evangelism through participation in a rhythm of life that says, 'let's share life together, and allow you room to experience God through a community living a spiritual rhythm'.

This form of evangelism is crucial in a culture fixated with consumerism. When so many people have no idea who they are, how are they ever going to know that they have a need for God? This was certainly part of my own experience, and I became a Christian because I was invited to share in the communal life of an emerging church. Many people are unaware that our consumerist market economy has created a society a bit like children in a sweet shop. Such a culture perpetuates our immaturity and our lack of deep human identity. In this context evangelism needs to begin with the transformational experience of deep human relations, to counteract the impoverishment of our somewhat adolescent human behaviour. Church then is called to be counter-cultural in how it models human identity, which, I hope, will enable us all to grow up somewhat.

So continuing in this calling for mission to be counter-cultural – what does it mean to engage with mission in a society dominated by the market? It necessitates the non-dualistic question I have already raised several times. 'How do we live in a market society, affirming what is good, yet not of a market society, challenging all that is oppressive and unjust?'

A Trinitarian-inspired church must act counter-culturally to the dehumanizing effects of the market. It is my contention that too many forms of church have colluded with a market society, so that mission becomes an attractional model of church, and the dominant motivation to reach out to people is to get them 'in' and attending church services. Mission activity is then reduced to institutional survival rather than the call to serve God unconditionally in the invisible Kingdom. Where a church prioritizes activity to get people through the doors there is a real danger of creating another form of consumerist choice, which is all about attracting the right people to the church. Very quickly this focuses on the rich and influential rather than the poor and dysfunctional, because the wealthy are able to pay more to keep the church going. I am not quite sure how this form of mission is either good news or transformative to wider society. Church is called to be a transformative, inclusive and justice-orientated community, seeking to make an impact in the place and network of relationships it is associated with. If mission is to happen it is going to be associated with risk and giving out in loving service to people with no expectation of having to start attending services on a Sunday. There should never be a 'mission risk assessment form' to avoid taking God-led and prayerfully discerned action. Mission by its nature is costly; it requires communities to focus on self-giving. It is no coincidence that the first thing that stops when a church community becomes unhealthy or institutionalized is mission.

However, when a church has an optimistic, risk-taking vision of balancing worship, mission and community, all focused on a Trinitarian ecclesiology, then it will be able to live a healthy Christian spirituality. Many new forms of church, inspired by the example of God as Trinity, are seeking to be this correction to unhealthy forms of religion. As forms of church they seek a radical re-connection with contemporary culture, which is by its nature post-Christendom, and post-secular.

At this point I want to mention the Anglican Communion's 'Marks of Mission', which I think are deeply challenging, inspiring and clearly based on a Trinitarian understanding of mission:

1 To proclaim the Good News of the Kingdom.
2 To teach, baptize and nurture new believers.
3 To respond to human need by loving service.

4 To seek to transform unjust structures of society.

5 To strive to safeguard the integrity of creation and sustain and renew the life of the earth.[4]

Most of this book has been about the needs of mission as numbered one to three above, with number three reflecting a Trinitarian focus on kenosis, or the self-giving of love to the world.

Generally the Church in the West has not been very good at mission priorities in the areas of four and five above. One of the strongest criticisms must be that justice has been too far down the list of priorities for the Church, and we forget that point three must relate to points four and five. We will have colluded with our market society and culture if we do not react counter-culturally to these distorting effects.

> The rich get richer, the poor get poorer, more and more species are driven to extinction, more toxins are released into our water and air and our overall quality of life is eroded.[5]

> Instead of globalizing the market and profit mechanisms, we need to globalize other cultural values, such as solidarity, collective compassion for victims, respect for cultures, sharing of goods, effective integration with nature, and feelings of humanity and mercy for the humiliated and offended.[6]

We need to remember that this mission is not only associated with people – but our planet too. We forget that the oppression of people is closely associated with environmental destruction. So

---

4 Bonds of Affection-1984 ACC-6, p. 49, Mission in a Broken World-1990 ACC-8, p.101.

5 Stephen B. Scharper, *National Catholic Reporter*, 8 September 1995, p. 24; 17 March 2000, p. 11.

6 Leonardo Boff, *Ecology and Liberation: A New Paradigm* (New York: Orbis Books, 1995), p. 105.

MISSION AS PARTICIPATION IN GOD

mission activity needs to be associated with social, economic and ecological justice.

It is no coincidence that the theologians who have explored ecological justice as an aspect of Christian mission have been contemplatives: monks, nuns and friars who are deeply Trinitarian in their thinking and acting. (Leonardo Boff, a key teacher in this area, is a Franciscan.) This is because the monastic model of church, which Avery Dulles calls the mystical communion model, was created by monks and nuns in reaction to the totalizing power of Christendom when Christianity was made the official religion of the Roman Empire.[7] Its ethos is counter-hierarchical and counter the false-self or ego, seeking to be a 'bottom up' fraternity – a community of those focused on mission as contemplative action, love of people and the world. Mission is only really possible when we are not deluded by personal greed, fear and anger. We remember that at the heart of a market society are the idols of greed, power and self-centredness. So the exponents of the monastic, mission-centred, Trinitarian and counter-cultural model are found throughout the history of the Church. They include Antony of Egypt, Francis and Clare of Assisi, Teresa of Avila and Benedict, as well as the lay monastic communities emerging out of the Protestant Reformation, including the Anabaptists and Shakers. And it is important to remember that the Protestant Reformation itself was driven by the monastic impulse to mission.[8] All these contributors sought to be radical communities, but maintained a connection to the wider Church. By participating in the *missio Dei*, many of these monastic-inspired communities changed the wider Church; their radical desire for mission combined following the Jesus of the Gospels with a high view of the Great Commission, and sought inspiration from the perfect expression of community in the Trinity.

---

7 Avery Dulles, *Models of the Church* (New York: Doubleday, 2002), pp. 44–53.

8 Jonathan Wilson-Hartgrove, 'A Vision So Old It Looks New', *Monasticism Old and New*, Christian Reflection, vol. 36, Baylor University, 2010, pp. 11–18.

True mission, then, is reliant on members of the Church living a healthy spiritual life in community. This is inspired by the perfect divine community of God, gathered in mutual love, justice, mercy and inclusion – and then sent into the world to express these attributes to the world. To do this effectively, the Church needs to follow the way of Christ, in powerlessness, unconditional love and self-giving service. We must learn from the mistakes of Christendom, that having privilege or power over people prevents effective mission:

> Within us there are instincts of violence, and desires to dominate, that distance us from benevolence in relation to life and nature . . . There is no need for anyone to be the ruler and to consider oneself independent, without needing others. Modern Cosmology teaches us that everything is related to everything else at all times, in all circumstances . . . It is important that we recuperate attitudes of respect and adoration of the Earth.[9]

In this more Trinitarian understanding of mission, salvation is about a restoration of full relationship between humanity and God, and also about human society's healthy stewardship of creation. As explored in an earlier chapter, the atonement, 'God putting things right', is about God dying and resurrecting for our anger rather than God's own anger. Jesus died to challenge the powers that distort and hold us back from our full humanity, to assist us to find again our common humanity in a deep love for God. We become angry because of our sin, or rather the thoughts that distort us, which are largely but not exclusively fear, pride, greed and self-centredness – attributes that are often considered healthy and desirable in a market society. So salvation is about God enabling us to be free from the thoughts that distort us, to live virtuously here and now, with the thoughts that give us life. This

---

9 Leonardo Boff, *Eco-Spirituality; Feeling, Loving and Thinking as Earth* in *Ecology: Cry of the Earth, Cry of the Poor* (New York: Orbis Books, 1997).

understanding of salvation is related to transformation, not just in the future of our human becoming (what I discussed earlier as *theosis*) but about becoming more human here and now. Christian discipleship, the call to contemplative action, is about facing the sins and thoughts that distort, through a balanced and contemplative spiritual life, sustained in the power and love of God. In the Moot Community, my current new monastic spiritual home, this understanding has been expressed as:

Virtues and the Thoughts that Distort Us

We live the rhythm of life by responding to the thoughts that distort by giving attention to the virtues that give us life.

	Virtues	Thoughts that distort
About the body	Moderation (Sobriety)	Gluttony (Intemperance)
	Chaste Love (Innocence)	Lust (Shamelessness)
	Generosity (Non-attachment)	Greed (Avarice)
About heart and mind	Patience (Serenity)	Anger (Impatience)
	Gladness	Sadness
	Courage	Fear (Anxiety)
	Spiritual Awareness	Spiritual Carelessness
About the human spirit	Magnanimity	Vanity
	Humility	Pride
	Honesty (Truthfulness)	Deceit (Untruth)

Thus salvation is not about us as individual consumers; on the contrary, God desires us to be saved from this individualistic distortion, finding fulfilment in belonging to and being formed by human community. This is why true Trinitarian-inspired mission is about the forming of ecclesial communities:

Since humanity is created in God's image and is called to share in God's fullness, the end of God's action is not that women and men are taken up individually; rather, like God in God's

innermost mystery, they too are formed into a community . . .
God is a community of Father, Son and Spirit, constantly involved in the world: salvation, human weakness, is life lived in
a community that reflects the community and self-giving that is
God . . . Active cooperation with God's mission binds women
and men closer to one another.[10]

Mission comes out of the life of a Christian community, from its
participation in the over-flowing of the Trinitarian life of God,
poured out into the world. The highpoint of this truth of the
Christian faith is expressed in Holy Communion or the Eucharist.
It is the missionary feast or meal of the Church. The Eucharist is
the recognition of the blessing of a gathered, Trinitarian-inspired
community, which shares in the body and blood of Jesus Christ
and is then sacramentally empowered and commissioned to be
sent into the world. The Eucharist is the reminder to Christians
of this calling, of God's sacramental presence in the world, and
the Church's commission to be sent and serve God in the world.
In this way the Eucharist is a deeply spiritually resourcing event,
where the participants of the community encounter and experience the Triune persons of God, and then go on to express this
love to the world in the ordinariness of their daily lives:

A Trinitarian-inspired ecclesiology speaks of the church as a
communion-in-mission. On the one hand, the church is understood as a communion; it is a people made one with the unity
of the Father, the Son, and the Holy Spirit . . . The Trinity challenges us to think differently not only about God but about ourselves. We are not so much individuals, as our Western culture
in particular would have it, but, as images of God, deeply social
and communal in nature. The perfect communication and self-
giving that is God's very self is the church's deepest reality, since

10 Bevans and Schroeder, *Constants in Context*, p. 287.

Christians have undergone *theosis* and participate in the divine nature.[11]

Thus mission is very much like the image of a participative dance that the Orthodox priest articulated at the beginning of this chapter. It is an image of the dynamism of God in mystical connection with humanity and the cosmos, which desires to see the common good being expressed in love. Drawing on all that we have explored, I finish with a summary of what I think are the attributes of a distinctly Trinitarian understanding of mission – as evangelism and just action:

- Deeply relational and personal.
- Generous and loving in service.
- Invitational and open, never controlling or seeking power over people.
- Responding to social, economic and ecological need.
- Passionate about God.
- Deep 'double listening' to God and to context, in prayer, before acting.
- Artistic and creative.
- Committed to an approach of catching up with what God is already seeking or doing.
- Committed to open up the salvation story as good news in non-threatening approaches, such as storytelling.
- Practitioners of contemplative Christianity, enabling spiritual questers to experience God for themselves.
- Providing a counter-narrative to the distortion of our market society of greed, privilege, power and self-centredness to sufficiency, wellbeing, powerlessness, self-care and self-giving.
- Seeking for transformation and justice in society and in people's spiritual lives.

---

11 Bevans and Schroeder, *Constants in Context*, p. 298.

10

Where from Here?

It was Immanuel Kant (1724–1804) who said:

> The doctrine of the Trinity provides nothing, absolutely noth-
> ing, of practical value, even if one claims to understand it; still
> less when one is convinced that it far surpasses our understand-
> ing . . . [it] offers absolutely no guidance for conduct.[1]

Clearly everything I have argued in this book so far is in opposition
to Kant's judgement of the Trinity. I believe that an understanding
of the Trinity as unity in diversity can profoundly help the Church
to learn a more nurturing and loving way to live together in difference. However, before we consider this, we need to face the issue
of leadership in the Church.

You may have noticed that until this point I haven't mentioned
anything about church leadership. I wanted to fully explore community first, and in my experience as soon as community is mentioned, ordination and leadership tend to dominate the discussion.
However, I do think Trinitarian ecclesiology presents a distinct
challenge to current understandings of leadership. Therefore we
must return to Augustine, the *filioque* clause and the doctrine of
the Trinity that we explored earlier.

Unfortunately, the consequence of Augustine's inclusion of the
filioque clause in the Nicene Creed was to create an internal hierarchy

---

1 C. A. Hall, *Learning Theology with the Church Fathers* (Leicester: IVP, 2002),
in B. Edgar, *The Message of the Trinity* (Leicester: IVP, 2004), pp. 22, 53.

within the nature of God. Theologians, including the current Pope Joseph Ratzinger, have drawn on the *filioque* clause to say that God the Father or Creator is more important than God the Son or Redeemer, and that both are more important than God the Holy Spirit or Sustainer. There is no evidence in scripture to support this hierarchy, and it is at odds with the Cappadocian Mothers' and Fathers' understanding of the Trinity. Nevertheless it proved very useful when justifying the power and office of the Pope in Rome. What was modelled by God should be imitated by the Church – or so it was argued. With this view of the Trinity, priests and bishops were not just important elements of administration, but the centre and life of the Church. For Volf, the episcopocentric model of the Church (endorsed by Ratzinger) is not consistent with a non-*filioque* version of the Nicene Creed:[2]

> Over the course of this investigation, I have tried to show (1) that the church is not a single subject, but rather a communion of interdependent subjects, (2) that the mediation of salvation occurs not only through office-holders, but also through all other members of the church, and (3) that the church is constituted by the Holy Spirit not so much by way of the institution of office as through a communal confession in which Christians speak the word of God to one another. From these three basic theological convictions, it follows that the life and structure of church cannot be episcopocentric. The church is not a monocentric-bipolar community, however articulated, but rather fundamentally, a polycentric community.[3]

For Volf, the laity is of equal importance to those who have a priestly office, because the gifts of the Holy Spirit are universal, and employed by the whole Church in service to the world:

---

2 M. Volf, *After Our Likeness: The Church as the Image of the Trinity* (Cambridge: Eerdmans, 1998), pp. 221–34.

3 *Ibid.*, p. 224.

Universal distribution of the charismata implies common responsibility for the life of the church. Such common responsibility is compatible with the particular charismata of leadership.
In the context of universal distribution of charismata, however,
such leadership acquires a new profile. It cannot be the task of
leaders, ordained or not, to do everything in the church themselves. This would lead to hypertrophy of this one member of
the body of Christ and to the fateful atrophy of all other members. The task of leaders is first to animate all the members of
the church to engage their pluriform charismatic activities, and
then to coordinate these activities.[4]

Here leadership is modelled in servant form, and is akin to coor-
dination, much like the role of the conductor of an orchestra or
the curator of an art gallery. The issue is in giving people room to
exercise their ministry accountably within the community. Much
of this learning has been appropriated by Emerging and Fresh
Expressions of church, with an emphasis on shared leadership,
or leadership by event. This model is centred on the participation of the whole Church – a deeply Trinitarian idea. Polycentric
communities are characterized by equality, which is distorted by
the implications of the *filioque* clause. This means that ordination,
and the offices of priest and bishop, are reframed by the context
of servant ministry. They may be offices of charismata and empowered by the Holy Spirit, but they are roles of function, not of
power, privilege or hierarchy.

Unsurprisingly this is not such a problem in the East, where
priests are seen as servants of the Church, and otherwise normal
people who can marry and have families. Bishops are seen as the wise
grandees of the Church, respected and listened to, but without the
power that is invested in Western bishops. It is important to remember that less than four hundred years ago, bishops in the Church of
England often had their own private armies! It is clear that if the

---

4 *Ibid.*, p. 230.

historic Western churches continue to endorse a purely hierarchical form of episcopocentric Church in a post-Christendom, disestablishmentarian period, the consequence will be that the laity will be further alienated and disempowered. As already discussed, some Emerging and Fresh Expressions of church have sought permission from their diocesan bishops to set up new monastic communities, with indigenous servant leadership. Some have appointed leaders by community election. These offices are modelled on service, not power. Leadership needs to be reframed as servanthood, with the function of empowering and nurturing the laity. This clearly models a Trinitarian-inspired way of being church, centred on unity in diversity.

If the global Church is to develop unity in diversity, an appreciation of Trinitarian ecclesiology is vital. This involves an approach modelled in the love of God, and seeking the full expression of humanity in all our difference. The core creedal statement of the Church as one, holy, catholic and apostolic, seems most applicable. This would mean that the world Church is fully present only when thinking about itself as Catholic and Protestant, conservative and liberal. Only together can the Church be fully church. If it could catch up with God's vision of its nature, the way it relates to the world and itself, it would be vastly improved. I have great admiration for Rowan Williams, the current Archbishop of Canterbury, for his extremely deep understanding and subtle appreciation of this. If he led in an episcopocentric way, he would attempt to use power politics to bring unity in conformity. He does not do this. Instead he is often silent in public, while working hard behind the scenes to help opposing forces meet and talk to each other. To some he has appeared weak, but for me it is clear that he seeks to serve the Church out of a vision of unity in diversity. He avoids Reformation-period Anglican history, when violent battles raged between rival claims to unity in conformity.

In this post-Christendom world, the vision of unity in diversity gives great insight into how the Church could move forward in a more relational way. As an alternative to fundamentalism, it enables an approach that has a high regard towards God and scripture, as well as to culture and being human. Some of this is being modelled in Emerging and Fresh Expressions of church, but there is still more need for a deep, authentic Christian spirituality in our post-secular age. As Volf says:

> A participative model of church requires more than just values and practices that correspond to participative institutions. The church is not first of all a realm of moral purposes; it is the anticipation, constituted by the presence of the Spirit of God, of the eschatological gathering of the entire people of God in communion with the triune God. Hence the church needs the vivifying presence of the Spirit, and without this presence, even a church with a decentralized participative structure and culture will become sterile, and perhaps more sterile even than a hierarchical church. For it will either have to operate with more subtle or open forms of coercion. Successful participative church life must be sustained by deep spirituality. Only the person who lives from the Spirit of communion (2 Corinthians 13.13) can participate authentically in the life of the ecclesial community.[5]

This hunger for deep spirituality is the inevitable consequence of our techno-consumer society. The great rise in spiritual tourism presents the challenge to the Church of whether it is willing to recognize the reality of this new context. Unfortunately there is an enormous amount of fear in churches, which have a tendency to look back rather than forwards. The increasingly fractured relations between evangelical and Catholic, conservative and liberal, across all denominations, exacerbates this sense of fear even more. Graham Cray put this well recently:

> Postmodern people are more likely to come to faith through experience which leads to understanding of doctrine than through

5 *Ibid.*, p. 257.

prior intellectual assent. But one of the tragedies of today is that some elements of the Church are now so firmly secularized in their disbelief in the supernatural that they have nothing to say to a culture which increasingly takes spirituality and the supernatural for granted.[6]

It appears to me that the Church in the West must engage with the task of exploring an authentic Christian spirituality that is able to connect with our current post-secular expression of new mysticism. The Deep Church and Emerging Church movements, though small, are significant responses to this challenge. However, with the greatest of respect, both are still minority sports in the UK church. Although Fresh Expressions has given permission for mission-centred experimental forms of church, it again has not birthed very many radical groups engaging with this brave new world. Additionally, many of those already in existence could be accused of being the same product, just with a little window-dressing.

One project that does model this unity in diversity model, and has a profound vision of engaging with the new mysticism, is St Andrew Holborn. Here a visionary vicar has drawn together a group of charismatic evangelicals, an Orthodox icon-making community, monks from Rome, and some Catholic Anglicans. All are very excited by this co-operation, sharing a strong sense of the participation of the Holy Spirit in their endeavour to put the *friar* back into the Blackfriars area of London. Already the church has become a place of visitation and pilgrimage. Underneath the church building is a natural well, which is proposed to be the site for a new healing centre. There is a shared understanding of perichoresis, kenosis and panentheism. If they get this mix right, it could be a great example of new, missional ecumenism engaging with new mysticism and spiritual tourism.

---

6 G. Cray, quoted in Y. Richmond *et al.*, *Evangelism in a Spiritual Age: Communicating Faith in a Changing Culture* (London: Church House Publishing, 2007), p. 14.

My hope for Emerging and Fresh Expressions of church is for the growth of new monasticism. I am excited by the thought of small contextual friaries, offering radical hospitality and access to a reframed Christian contemplative tradition, growing up all around the country. However, the movement needs a contemporary incarnation of Evelyn Underhill (a Christian mystic of the early twentieth century) to bring this spirituality to life in the twenty-first century. Many of the new monastic groups are attempting to set up intentional, residential communities, with radical hospitality through café church, arts, alternative worship and contemplative patterns of prayer and meditation. Though few in number, some have taken root in various locations in the UK. It is my own personal hope that the potent combination of innovative hospitality and a spiritual patterning of life will allow people to directly experience God.

A fictional example of this hope is expressed in a story by Ian Cron. It revolves around Kenny, who has a stress-related breakdown. Following the death of a young girl, he begins to seek God for wholeness and acceptance. In his quest he studies St Francis, learning from the original Christian friars about life. The story's climax centres around the experience of God through the Eucharist:

Kenny had a sense of the poetic. He took us to a six o'clock Mass in one of the side chapels at Saint John Lateran. It was only fitting that our last stop would be at the site where the Franciscan Order had received a blessing from the pope to minister to the world . . . when we knelt at the altar to receive Communion, all of my confidence quickly withered. When the elderly priest came to me, I held out my cupped hands to receive the communion host. The old priest, however, suffered from a slight tremor in his hands, so I had to keep moving my own to try and position them under his to receive the round wafer . . . Just when it looked like the exchange might end happily, . . . the wafer fell between the cracks of my coupled hands and hit the stone floor of the altar in front of me . . . I froze. I had fumbled Jesus.

God bless that palsied old priest. Without so much as skipping a beat, he reverently picked up the host, held it to heaven, and murmured, 'Veni, veni, Sancte Spiritu', then closed his eyes and received it himself. He took another wafer from the communion paten and waveringly placed it securely in the nest formed by my outstretched hands. Gazing deeply into my eyes, he said 'My son, this is the body of Christ.' What happened next is difficult to explain and perhaps, as with all mysteries, it is unwise to try. All I know is that in the moment of reception I was visited by God. Perhaps it was the goodness of the priest and his graciousness that silently opened a portal through which I momentarily made contact with the divine life. Or maybe it was the Eucharist itself – the host mingling with my brokenness, dissolving in saliva, coming to rest in the shallows of my heart's confusion. Kneeling at the altar, I was overwhelmed by the sense that my fragmented and discontinuous life actually made sense.[7]

This profound sense of transcendent encounter with God is what the Church must strive to model. I believe it can come through manifold traditions – contemplative prayer, silence, charismatic worship – you name it, God can use it. The key thing is confidence in the Church and in God that such things are possible. A change in skill sets for leaders of the Church will be required. The practice of contemplative prayer has been seen as optional for church leaders. I would argue that in the context of a culture of new mysticism and spiritual tourism, it is essential. All trained leaders need to have good group listening and facilitation skills, the ability to enable and inspire – all these are essential. Leaders ought also to be familiar with the ancient traditions of the Church, considering themselves custodians of it, so as to enable post-secular pilgrims to learn of its richness. In other words, this means being able to support a focus on ancient:future practice, reframing resources of

---

7 Ian Morgan Cron, *Chasing Francis* (Colorado Springs: Navpress, 2006), pp. 177–8.

the past into the contemporary context. Many have done just this
with labyrinth prayer walks, contemplative prayer, chanting and
stations of the cross. There are many ancient media that effectively
enable encounter with the Triune God. It is all down to the imagination and creativity of the Church.

The greatest challenge remains this: how do we be church in
a consumerist, technological, business-oriented world? I am concerned about the lack of knowledge of the faith many Christians
seem to suffer from. There is a tribal attitude, now very en-
trenched, where one's Christian identity is defined by how we are
'not like them'. I am also concerned that many churches operate on essentially the same terms as corporate business. It hit me
quite recently that such forms of church tend to downplay the
values of Trinitarian ecclesiology and an understanding of unity
in diversity.

The models explored in Avery Dulles's insightful book *Models
of Church* are a reflection of the varied emphases placed on the
person of Christ. Briefly, the models, and their ecclesiastical corol-
laries, are as follows: God as King – church as political society; God
as Trinity – church as mystical communion; God as Sacramental –
church as sacrament; God as Servant – church as servant; God
as Proclaimer – church as herald; and finally, God as teacher –
church as discipler. These are pretty well known, and I have already covered the Church as mystical communion and sacrament
models in this book. I would like to add another model, the increasing presence of which deeply troubles me, mainly because I
don't believe its consequences have been thought through. It is the
Church as business model. It seems to have seeped in with little
questioning, due to the financial pressures of the modern world.
As far I am aware there is as yet very little written about it, even
though very many churches have absorbed the approach. Clearly
this model is not based on the significance of Christ, but purely on
business practice.

I am concerned that it does not foster a high view of church as
an alternative, inclusive community. Instead the emphasis is on

something of a process model. In my experience, the PCC of a church like this quickly becomes the board, congregants become shareholders, and the church becomes divided into various departments sustaining different business activities. Where is the place of the poor in this model? Can those of little economic or work value find a place here? And what of those without business skills? For me this is of much greater concern to the Church at large than the hot-potato issues, such as sexuality and gender, that these churches often champion. So why is the Church silent on this issue?

In some ways I trace the development of alternative worship and the Emerging Church as a reaction to churches that were increasingly dehumanizing in their business approach – they had made the shift from fluid community to organization. I would argue that many of the 'successful' churches in London are built on a model of church as business, and that they visibly demonstrate its weakness. The question needs to be asked how, if they are to be contextual and authentic, are these churches being in but not of business culture? I think many of us who have been part of such churches have a sorry tale to tell. Vicars seem to operate as powerful managing directors with significant financial and political power. The danger of distortion to the function of the body of Christ is substantial.

Don't get me wrong: I am not against business innovation or the need for creative entrepreneurship where it is considered and used wisely. However, I am concerned that many do not seem to be aware of the consequences of taking on capitalist and business models of the Church. For me, the greatest downside is that the mission activities of such churches cannot be counter to business values. They target the powerful, rich and successful, avoiding the poor and the disadvantaged, and have a very Christendom-focused approach to both church and mission.

The mystical communion model, coupled with the sacramental model, is the form of church required to counter the syncretism of church as business. Our challenge in the twenty-first century is to re-engage with the poor, who are increasingly excluded from a society defined by consumerism and technology. If anything, predictions appear to suggest that society will further fragment between the 'haves' and the 'have nots'. Where will the Church be? Will it seek to engage with the bored youth on our streets who have nothing to do and nowhere to go? It seems that extremism and hate have found a breeding ground among the poor, so it is vital that the Church gets its hands dirty by engaging with both socio-economic extremes. After all, is this not where Christ, by the Holy Spirit, will draw us?

All this aside, I am optimistic that a contemporary form of deep spirituality, which can draw together the historic traditions and bring the heart of the faith to our contemporary culture, is now taking shape. Via a model of unity in diversity, renewed transcendence, and the mystical transformation of encounter with the Trinity, it will bring hope and real encounter back to our world.

> The Trinity is the source of mission because the sending of the church into the world is a continuation of the Father's love which led to a sending of the Son and Spirit, Trinitarian love (not fear, obligation or duty) is what lies at the heart of Christian mission (Matthew 28:19).[8]

So how do we maintain this deep spirituality in the West? How do we sustain a stronger Trinitarian theology and ecclesiology?

I return to Peter Rollins, the Emerging Church and the language of icons:

> Those within the emerging conversation find unity not by a type of cloning which all Christians are encouraged to believe the same thing . . . speaking of God is but only ever speaking about our understanding of God . . . this approach diligently maintains a conceptual distance between ourselves and God,

---

8 Edgar, *The Message of the Trinity*, p. 29.

one which approaches the divine mystery as something to be transformed by rather than solved by . . .[9]

To treat something as an icon is to view particular words, images or experiences as aids in contemplation of that which cannot be reduced to words, images or experience. Not only this, but the icon represents a place where God touches humanity. Consequently, icons are only the place where we contemplate God, they also act as the place that God uses in order to communicate with us . . . In this iconic understanding, our thoughts concerning God are directed towards God in love rather than enslaving God with words.[10]

There is great wisdom in these words. We must pursue a form of faith that holds in tension knowing and not knowing, with an emphasis on trans-rational knowledge of God through contemplative forms of prayer and worship. Maybe having an awareness of the potential idolatry of words frees both us and God. I am convinced that the combination of this understanding of the Triune God and the disciplines of contemplative prayer, action and worship will help the Christian faith to rediscover its full place in society. To do this, the Church must develop a language and practices that relate to our consumerist and technological culture. However, there must also be a commitment to transcend the weaknesses of Western theological thinking, some of which I have outlined here.

So I finish where I started, remembering the insights of the Emerging and Fresh Expressions of church: we must not misuse our understandings of the Trinity to project fixed understandings onto God. Trinitarianism is an imperfect understanding drawing on the spiritual experiences of people with the One God in three persons. However, it is, in my opinion, the best construct among

---

9 P. Rollins, *How (not) to Speak of God* (London: SPCK, 2006), p. 32.

10 *Ibid.*, pp. 38, 40.

other imperfect constructs, and a distinctive understanding that can root us deeply in God.

Instead we must remember that theology is the place where God speaks into human discourse, and that as we do mission, we point people to the Divine. Religious truth is that which transforms reality rather than that which describes it. In worship and mission we seek to contemplate God, who in turn touches and communicates with humanity. If the Church is truly modelled on this approach, it will meet deeply with contemporary culture. And maybe for the first time, churches of all different traditions will truly model unity in diversity.

Instead of more theory, the following chapter is reserved for prayer, contemplation and worship. I encourage you to seek God as you consider the issues covered in this book. Thank you for journeying with me.

11

Trinitarian Devotions

This section includes a number of poems and devotionals to promote exploration through imaginative encounter.

Perichoresis – The Divine Dance of God

Ian Mobsby

Heads bowing, hands sharing, hearts racing
Feet poised suspended in the support of the other.
Holy Three yet one, laugh, cry, celebrate and lament their co-creativity.

Time burst out as the by-product of a hurling helix
of mystical presence
swaying through the dance.
Life and all things became real
Out of the dynamic of joy and love expressed in movement.

The Creator led the dance from beginning to incarnation,
The Redeemer led the dance from incarnation to Pentecost
The Companion leads the dance now from the time of the church
to the consummation.
But Holy dance
don't slow down,
don't wait on us inattentive humanity.

Free us Holy Three in one to learn the dance
Teach us to be free from our selfishness and greed
Let us relearn how to dance spiritually
And be a blessing to the Cosmos
And be the spiritual community
The dancing God calls us to be

Amen

Periochoresis

Pádraig Ó Tuama

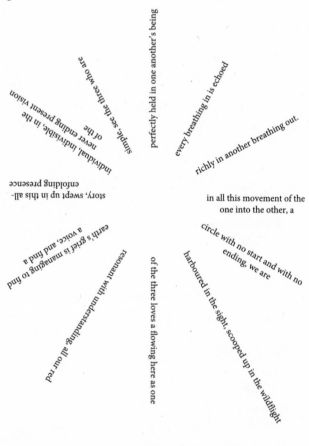

perfectly held in one another's being
every breathing in is echoed
richly in another breathing out.
in all this movement of the one into the other, a
circle with no start and with no ending, we are
harboured in the sight, scooped up in the wildflight
of the three loves a flowing here as one
resonant with understanding, all our red
earth's grief is managing to find a voice, and find a
story, swept up in this all-enfolding presence
Individual, invisible, in the never ending present vision
simple, see the three who are

Perichoresis

Michael L. Radcliffe

On Friday nights we went to clubs
until we noticed something that
night when the three of them came and took
over the regular dancing. So

Did the Creator throw shapes on the
dance floor whilst dancing a salsa that
turned all the heads of the punters there?

Vogueing away while the other two
scattered. They took up their places but
somehow remaining together there

How the Companion perfected that
fight in a way that was calming them.
Making them friends from thereon until

Now. The Revealer is reveling
showing us all just a little too
much how its done by his lead for us

Dancing together while beckoning onlookers
come on and join us, and have a good
time. Doesn't matter it's happening.

Keeping the rhythm up copying
maybe looked easy as no-one would
dare to reject their advances then
in pairs we couldn't make it work
and groups of us tried sussing out

as individuals put together
were fitting triplets into four time.

We stopped the dancing, getting going
on paper noting down what happened
as dancing disappeared while writing
and scrapping round some bits of paper.

Moot Icon – The Trinity

Michael L. Radcliffe

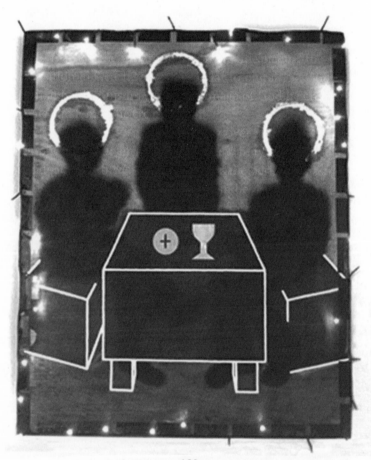

Isaac Laughed

Bowie Snodgrass

First Sarah laughed –
When three angels said
She would bear a son.
Even in my old age?!

Then Isaac laughed,
Going along with his dad,
Sure, we'll do the sacrifice,
I will journey with you.

So Abraham took him,
Set him on an altar –
When an angel appeared
From God and laughed.

Take Your Place

Tara Lamont Eastman

This hunger that draws me closer to You.
This thirst that brings me back to Truth.
Where can these needs elsewhere be met?
Sifting through the shallow,
This pushes past the rest.

The Bread, the Wine –
made real in time.
The Body, the Blood –
fills my needs in love.

GOD UNKNOWN

Cups to fill,
Bread to break –
Each day holds a Eucharist . . .
Take your place.

Brought together in one place,
We all are drawn by Your grace.
All as one and each one seen –
How does this table draws us?
So unpredictable and unclean.

The Bread, the Wine –
made real in time.
The Body, the Blood –
fills my needs in love.

Cups to fill,
Bread to break –
Each day holds a Eucharist . . .
Take your place.

Carry this meal to the heart of the world.
Carry the message of hope restored.
Sit and share this meal and rest –
Forgiveness offered, conversation blessed.

The Bread, the Wine –
made real in time.
The Body, the Blood –
fills my needs in love.

Cups to fill,
Bread to break –
Each day holds a Eucharist . . .
Take your place.

TRINITARIAN DEVOTIONS

Cups to fill,
Bread to break –
Each day holds a Eucharist . . .
Take your place.

Recommended Reading

This book is part of an ongoing conversation within Emerging and Fresh Expressions of church. I therefore recommend the following books to read as part of the journey.

Ryan Bolger, *Emerging Churches: Creating Christian Communities in Postmodern Cultures*, London: SPCK, 2006.

Luke Bretherton and Andrew Walker, *Recovering Deep Church in Remembering our Future*, London: Paternoster Press, 2007.

Kester Brewin, *The Complex Christ*, London: SPCK, 2004.

John Caputo, *On Religion* (Thinking in Action), New York: Routledge, 2001.

Graham Cray, Ian Mobsby and Aaron Kennedy (eds), *New Monasticism as Fresh Expressions of Church*, Norwich: Canterbury Press, 2010.

Steven Croft and Ian Mobsby (eds), *Ancient Faith Future Mission: Fresh Expressions in the Sacramental Tradition*, Norwich: Canterbury Press, 2008.

Ian Mobsby, *Emerging and Fresh Expressions of Church*, London: Moot Community Publishing, 2007.

RECOMMENDED READING

Mike Riddell, *Threshold to the Future*, London: SPCK, 1998.

Peter Rollins, *How (Not) to Speak of God*, London: SPCK, 2006.

Peter Rollins, *The Fidelity of Betrayal*, London: SPCK, 2008.

Richard Sudworth, *Distinctly Welcoming*, Bletchley: Scripture Union, 2007.